BEZAUBERNDE PUPPENREISE

ENCHANTED JOURNEY

BEZAUBERNDE PUPPENREISE
ENCHANTED JOURNEY

PUPPEN VON HILDEGARD GÜNZEL
DOLLS BY HILDEGARD GÜNZEL
1972-1997
TEXT VON KARIN SCHREY

Verlag Puppen & Spielzeug

Fotos:
Bruno Kapahnke: Seiten 9, 13, 15, 18, 19, 22, 24, 25, 26, 27, 31, 34, 35, 37, 38, 40, 43, 46, 47, 48, 49, 51, 52,
53, 55, 56, 58, 59, 60, 61, 62, 63, 65, 66, 67, 68, 69, 70, 72, 74, 75, 76, 77, 78, 79,84
Jean Lacasse: Titelfoto, Seiten 16, 86, 87, 88, 90, 93, 95, 97
Birgitte Völker: Seiten 71, 73, 81, 83
Gert Wohlfarth: Seite 54
Nick Rosenberg: Seite 85
Archiv H. Günzel: Seiten 6, 7, 8, 10, 21, 29, 32, 33, 36, 39, 42, 45, 64
Die Fotos von Seite 100-114 entstammen den jeweiligen Firmenarchiven.
Titelfoto: Pandora,
Porzellan mit Wachs überzogen
lim. Ed. 25 USA, 25 Europa
89 cm groß

Die deutsche Bibliothek - CIP-Einheitsaufnahme
Günzel, Hildegard:
Bezaubernde Puppenreise:
Puppen von Hildegard Günzel 1972 - 1997 / Hildegard
Günzel, Karin Schrey - Duisburg:
Verlag Puppen und Spielzeug, 1997
ISBN 3-87463-253-9
NE: Schrey, Karin (Mitarb.)

Copyright 1997 by
GERT WOHLFARTH GmbH
Verlag Fachtechnik + Mercator-Verlag
Verlag Puppen & Spielzeug, Duisburg
ISBN 3-87463-253-9

Nostalgie - und erste Puppen 1972 - 1980
Nostalgia and the first dolls 1972-1980

Fünfundzwanzig Jahre sind eine lange Zeit. Der vierte Teil von einem Jahrhundert. Seit fünfundzwanzig Jahren gibt es sie nun schon: Puppen von Hildegard Günzel. Wie kam es dazu? Was veranlaßte eine junge Frau Anfang der siebziger Jahre, Puppen zu machen? Wie war das damals, als alles anfing? Wie kam es überhaupt zu dem enormen Interesse, das Puppen bei so vielen Menschen weltweit finden? Und wie hat sich die „Szene" entwickelt? Wer waren die Menschen, die mit ihren Anfängen verknüpft sind?

Dieses Buch erzählt den Werdegang Hildegard Günzels und natürlich den ihrer Puppen, die heute Freunde auf der ganzen Welt haben. Doch darüber hinaus berührt es die Schicksale vieler Menschen, die mit eben diesem Werdegang verbunden sind. Viele von ihnen, die es lesen, werden sich erinnern: mit Vergnügen, aber vielleicht auch mit ein wenig Wehmut. Denn einige ihrer Weggefährten sind heute schon nicht mehr am Leben. Fünfundzwanzig Jahre sind eine lange Zeit. Und doch erscheinen sie uns sehr kurz. „Was?" werden Sie sich beim Lesen der einen oder anderen Begebenheit vielleicht ungläubig fragen, „so lange ist das schon her? Kaum zu glauben!" Menschen vergessen vieles. Zum Glück. Doch mitunter vergessen wir auch Menschen, Dinge (ja, auch Puppen) und Erlebnisse, die wir eigentlich in Erinnerung behalten wollten. Deshalb ist es nun an der Zeit, inne zu halten und zurückzuschauen.

„Das Schönste, was wir in der Vergangenheit antreffen, ist die Hoffnung", sagte einst ein bedeutender deutscher Dichter des 18. Jahrhunderts. 1945, in dem Jahr, in dem Hildegard Günzel geboren wurde, war Hoffnung das einzige, was geblieben war. Die Welt war verstört, zerstört waren die deutschen Städte. Niemand hätte sich damals träumen lassen, daß es schon bald wieder eine Zeit des Wohl-

Twenty five years is a long time. A quarter of a century. They have been around now for twenty-five years, dolls by Hildegard Günzel that is. How did this come about? What prompted a young lady to make dolls at the beginning of the 1970s? What was it like when it all started? What brought about the enormous interest in dolls shown by people throughout the world? And how has this „scene" developed? Who were the people associated with her beginnings? This books narrates the career of Hildegard Günzel and naturally that of her dolls, who today have friends from the four corners of the earth. But more than this, it concerns the destiny of many people associated with precisely the career which this book is about. Many of you who read it will remember with pleasure, but also with a little nostalgia perhaps, since some of Hildegard Günzel's erstwhile companions are, even today, no longer with us. Twenty-five years is a long time. And yet it seems to have passed very quickly. „What !" you will perhaps ask incredulously, when reading about one or the other event, „Did that really happen so long ago? That's hardly believable". People forget a great deal. Fortunately. But sometimes we also forget people, things (indeed even dolls) and experiences which we actually wanted to retain in our memory. It is for this reason that it is now time to pause, take stock, and reflect. „The most beautiful thing that we come across in the past is hope" once said a great German writer in the eighteenth century. In 1945, the year in which Hildegard Günzel was born, hope was the only thing which remained. The world was bewildered. The cities of Germany were destroyed. At that time no one would ever have dreamed that there would ever be a time of prosperity and peace again soon, in which enemies have become friends. That there would be a time in

stands und des Friedens geben würde, in der aus Feinden Freunde geworden waren. Daß es eine Zeit geben würde, in der Frauen (und sogar Männer!) sich damit beschäftigen würden, Puppen zu machen. Und dies nur zum eigenen Vergnügen. Denn so fing es an: es war reine Freude am Gestalten, die die ersten Puppenkünstler zu ihrer Arbeit antrieb. Sie hatten keine unmittelbaren Vorbilder. Zwar hat Puppenmachen in Deutschland eine lange und große Tradition - doch Traditionen hatten nach dem Krieg einen zu bitteren Beigeschmack, als daß man sich gern auf sie besonnen hätte. Erst, als sich die ersten Puppenkünstler mit Ausstellungen an die Öffentlichkeit wagten, entdeckte man sie wieder: Natürlich, hieß es dann, da gab es doch damals, 1908 in München, eine Bewegung...

Damals entstanden die ersten Künstlerpuppen, entworfen von berühmten Frauen: Marion Gräfin Kaulitz und Marie Marc-Schnür, der Ehefrau von Franz Marc, des vielleicht berühmtesten Mitglieds des „Blauen Reiters", einer Vereinigung avangardistischer Künstler. Ihre Geschöpfe lösten den ersten Künstlerpuppenboom der Geschichte aus. Doch so unvermittelt, wie es uns heute erscheint, entstand auch diese erste „Szene" nicht. Puppensammeln und Puppenmachen war zur Zeit der Jahrhundertwende ein beliebtes Hobby der Damen der Gesellschaft. Damit es in Nachkriegs-Deutschland überhaupt zu einer Sammlerszene kommen konnte, mußte es erst wieder so etwas wie eine Gesellschaft geben.

Mit dem beginnenden „Wirtschaftswunder" Anfang der sechziger Jahre waren die Rahmenbedingungen für das Entstehen einer Puppenszene schon wieder geschaffen. 1961 war Hildegard Günzel sechzehn Jahre alt und absolvierte das erste Jahr ihres Design-Studiums an der Deutschen Meisterschule für Mode in München, die sie 1965, mit dem Diplom als Modedesignerin und Grafikerin in der Tasche, verließ. Danach arbeitete sie als freie Mode- und Schmuckdesignerin für verschiedene Firmen.

6

Erste Puppe für Sohn Kai, Kopf, Arme und Beine aus Gips, Kleid und Hut von Hildegard Günzels Mutter, Lydia Gehrig, 1972.
First doll for son Kai. Head, arms and legs are made of plaster. Dress and hat made by Hildegard Günzel's mother Lydia Gehrig, 1972.

which women (and even men!) would occupy themselves by making dolls. And this simply for their own pleasure. This is how it began. It was the pure pleasure of creation which drove the first doll artists to take up this work. They had no first-hand examples to follow. Admittedly, doll-making has a long and rich tradition in Germany - but after the war the associations of tradition were too bitter to the palate for people to think kindly of them. Only when the first doll artists ventured forth before the public gaze by staging exhibitions, was tradition rediscovered. Of course, then it was said that there was a movement in Munich in 1908 wasn't there? It was at this time that the first artistic dolls came into being, created by famous ladies, Marion Countess Kaulitz and Marie Marc-Schnür, wife of Franz Marc, who was perhaps the most famous member of the „Blaue Reiter" associa-

Die späten Sechziger waren die Zeit der Hippiebewegung: Florale Muster dominierten. Begriffe wie flower power, „make love not war", Woodstock kennzeichnen das Lebensgefühl einer Jugend, die grenzenlos war: Sie überschritt Grenzen unterschiedlichster Art,

oben und rechts: Arbeiten aus der Deutschen Meisterschule für Mode.
Top and right. Work from the German Master School of Fashion, Design.

nicht nur politische. Die Jugend hatte genug von Kriegen, von heißen wie von kalten. Ein bis dahin nie gekanntes Solidaritätsgefühl vereinte weltweit alle „unter dreißig". Martin Luther Kings „I have a dream..." könnte als der Leitsatz der damaligen Jugend gelten. Doch die Welt der Erwachsenen war nicht reif für diese Jugend. Pablo Picasso sagte einmal: „Es dauert lange, bis man jung wird!" So lange wollte die damalige Jugend nicht warten. Enttäuscht wandte sie sich ab. Nach innen. Einem wieder rauher gewordenen politischen Klima setzte die Jugend eine neue Innerlichkeit entgegen. Die Philosophien der westlichen Welt hatten sich in ihren Augen alle als nicht „wahr" erwiesen. Die Jugend suchte nun die „Wahrheit" überwiegend in östlichen Kulturen, in den Weisheiten Buddhas und den Lehren indischer Gurus. Indien war für viele das Land der Sehnsüchte, Indienkleider waren

tion of avant-garde artists. Their creation gave rise to the first artistic doll boom in history. But even this first „scene" was not as abrupt as it appears to us today. Doll-collecting and doll-making was a popular hobby of society ladies at the turn of the century. For there to be a doll-collectors scene in post-war Germany at all, there first of all had to be something akin to a society. The background conditions for a doll-scene to come into being were established once more with the beginning of the 'economic miracle' of the early 1960s. In 1961 Hildegard Günzel was sixteen years old and was completing the first year of her design course at the German School for Fashion Tailoring and Designing in Munich, which she finished in 1965 with a degree in Fashion Design and Graphic Art under her belt. Following that she worked for various companies on a freelance basis as a fashion and jewellery designer. The late sixties were the era of the hippy movement; floral patterns dominated. Slogans such as 'flower power', 'make love not war', 'Woodstock', are typical of the joie de vivre of a young generation which knew no bounds. It transgressed all kinds of limits, not only political ones. Young people had had enough of wars, fierce wars as well as cold wars. A feeling of solidarity hitherto unknown united all those „under thirties" across the globe. Martin Luther King's „I have a dream....." could have been the guiding principle of the younger generation of the day. But the world of adults was not ready for this young generation. Pablo Picasso once said, „It takes a long time to become young"! The young generation of that era did not want to wait that long. Disappointed, they drifted away. Inwards. The younger generation confronted the a political climate which had become harsher with a new spirituality. In their eyes the philosophies of the western world had all turned out to be „untrue". The younger generation now sought the 'truth', predominantly in eastern cultures, in the wisdom of Buddha and the teachings of Indian

7

„in". Dazu passten lange Haare, die geschmückt werden konnten. Auch Hildegard Günzel trug sie gerne. Dazu entwarf sie Haarschmuck. Noch in den frühen achtziger Jahren wurden ihre Haarperlen von vielen Frauen gern getragen.

Die siebziger Jahre brachten auch, als Spätfolge der Hippiebewegung, eine Rückbesinnung auf „Natürlichkeit". Die Ökowelle begann zu rollen, „Bio" war das neue Schlagwort. Man begann, beim Einkaufen nach „naturbelassenen" Lebensmitteln zu fragen. Man trug Baumwolle und viel Handgestricktes aus pflanzensaftgefärbter Wolle. Auf dem Fußboden lagen Reisstroh- und Schafwollteppiche. Dazu paßten auch die glatten, „modernen" Möbel der späten Sechziger nicht mehr. Nostalgisches war gefragt. Omas Spitzendeckchen lagen nun sogar in Studentenbuden auf der Kommode vom Sperrmüll. Glücklich konnte sich schätzen, wer ältere Verwandte besaß, die sich gern von ihren alten - bis dahin von den Jungen schnöde mißachteten - Möbeln trennten. Andere mußten in die Trödelläden oder auf den Flohmarkt gehen, um die begehrten Weichholzschränke zu erwerben, die meistens dunkel gebeizt oder gestrichen waren. Sie wurden abgelaugt und „naturbelassen" mit Gegenständen dekoriert, die man gleichfalls auf dem Flohmarkt oder im Antiquitätengeschäft erstanden hatte: So kam es zur ersten - oder besser: Wiederbegegnung Hildegard Günzels mit Puppen.

Eines Tages, bei einem Besuch bei Freunden, stand sie fasziniert vor einem alten Weichholzschrank mit antiken Puppen, die damals auch plötzlich auf Flohmärkten auftauchten. Zwar waren die Preise Anfang der siebziger Jahre nicht mit denen von heute zu vergleichen,

Entwurf eines Modeschmucks, hier Haarperlen, die man auf- und zuklappen kann.
Design for fashion-jewellery. Here, hair-pearls which can be snapped open and closed.

gurus. Many longed to visit India, Indian clothing was „in". Even Hildegard Günzel liked wearing them. Together with garments from the sub-continent went long hair, which could be adorned. Hildegard Günzel designed hair ornaments. Even up to the early 1980s many women still liked wearing her hair pearls. As a belated consequence of the hippy-movement, the seventies heralded the return to „naturalness". The ecology wave began to surge. „Bio" was the new catch phrase. When shopping, people began to ask for „additive-free" foodstuffs. People began to wear clothing made of cotton and lots of hand-knitted garments made of wool coloured with plant-dyes. Coir matting and sheep's wool carpets lay on the

doch junge Menschen Mitte zwanzig konnten sie sich dennoch nicht leisten. Andere Dinge waren wichtiger. Die Familie ging vor. Doch Hildegard Günzels „Kinderseele" (Günzel) fühlte sich von den aparten Geschöpfen angesprochen. Sie brachten etwas in ihr zum Klingen. Fast vergessene Gefühle stiegen aus der Tiefe des Unterbewußtseins empor. Sie erinnerten sie an die Tage ihrer Kindheit, als sie ihren Puppenwagen an der Stadtmauer ihrer romantischen Heimatstadt Tauberbischofsheim entlang schob. In ihr entstand der Wunsch, auch eine Puppensammlung zu besitzen. Doch wie kommt man dazu - ohne Geld? Aber - war sie denn keine Künstlerin? Hatte sie nicht ihr Design-Studium mit Diplom absolviert? „Da ich mir keine alten Puppen kaufen konnte, beschloß ich, mir selbst welche zu machen". Dies war der Anstoß zur eigenen Kreativität, der den Stein ins Rollen brachte. Das Gleiche geschah, Jahrzehnte zuvor, auch einer anderen berühmten deutschen Puppenmacherin, Käthe Kruse, und Jahre später sollte es Hildegard Günzel auch von anderen Frauen, die Puppen machen, immer wieder hören. Zunächst jedoch kaufte sie sich den ersehnten Weichholzschrank. Da war noch keine Puppe da, die sie hätte hineinsetzen können.

Doch bald danach, 1972, gab es sie: die erste Günzel-Puppe! Sie hatte einen Gipskopf mit großen Augen und Beine mit angeformten Schuhen. Ein Problem waren die Kleider. Das lag jedoch nicht am Können, sondern am Wollen. Die Puppenmacherin hatte schon immer eine Abneigung gegen das Nähen. Kleider entwerfen ja, das macht sie mit Begeisterung, da schwelgt sie geradezu in Stoffen, Spitzen und Bändern. Doch umsetzen sollte ihre Ideen tunlichst jemand anders. Heute sind es Spezialisten, die für die Garderobe der Günzel-Puppen verantwortlich sind. Damals, 1972, mußte sie noch alles selbst machen. Doch die Begierde, die fertige Puppe vor sich zu sehen, erleichterte auch diese Arbeit.

Die ersten Marionetten und Puppen in Cernit, 1973.
The first puppets and dolls in cernit, 1973.

DIGITAL RECORDING

DECCA

Rossini · Respighi
La Boutique Fantasque
Britten · Rossini
**Soirées Musicales
Matinées Musicales**
National Philharmonic Orchestra
Richard Bonynge

Cernit-Fantasiepuppe aus den späten 70ger Jahren, hier als „Star" auf einer Plattenhülle.

Cernit fantasy doll from the late 1970's, here as a "star" on a record cover.

Mit der ersten Puppe begann die Suche nach der vollkommenen Form. Und damit verbunden die Suche nach dem dafür am besten geeigneten Material, mit dem sich die Vorstellungen der Künstlerin umsetzen ließen. Damals gab es noch keine Firmen für Puppenbedarf. Wer damals erzählt hätte, er machte Puppen, begegnete allenfalls Erstaunen. Schlimmstenfalls wurde man müde belächelt. Wie? Eine erwachsene Frau beschäftigt sich mit solchem Kinderkram? Etwa zwei Jahre hatte Hildegard Günzel experimentiert, als ihr in der Firma, für die sie Bastelanleitungen schrieb, der erste Block Cernit in die Hände fiel. Die

floor. Even the smooth „modern" furniture of the late sixties no longer fitted in. Nostalgic artefacts were what was wanted now. Grandmother's lace doilies were even decorating the top of the chest of drawers which had been rescued from the tip but were now gracing students' rooms. Those who had older relatives who were happy to part with their old furniture - which up until then had been disdainfully scorned by the younger generation - counted themselves lucky. Others had to go to the second-hand shops or to the flea markets to get hold of the coveted pine furniture, which was mostly painted or stained in dark

Geschmeidigkeit des Materials, seine Formbarkeit und leichte Anwendbarkeit und nicht zuletzt der wachsartige Schimmer, den Gegenstände aus Cernit aufweisen, führten dazu, daß aus dem Puppen-Hobby Hildegard Günzels eine Profession wurde. Nach und nach entdeckte sie die vielfältigen Möglichkeiten, die Cernit ihr bot. Die ersten von ihr gefertigten Püppchen waren Anhänger. Es waren kleine, stilisierte Frauenfiguren mit - shocking! - angedeutetem Busen. Man konnte sie an einem Lederband um den Hals tragen. Sie paßten hervorragend zu Indien- und Hippiekleidern, doch genauso gut zu Jeans und darüber hinaus zu einem neuen feministischen Selbstbewußtsein der jungen, modernen Frauen, wie es die Zeitschrift „Emma" propagierte, zu deren eifrigen Leserinnen auch Hildegard Günzel damals gehörte.

Irgendwann wurden die Anhänger immer größer und schwerer, „bis man sie sich nicht mehr um den Hals hängen konnte". Unversehens hatten sie sich in Marionetten verwandelt. Glaubte die Künstlerin, daß sich ihre Puppenleidenschaft leichter beherrschen ließe, so lange sie ihre Puppen am Gängelband führte? Vielleicht. Doch schließlich ließ sie sie doch von der Leine. Den ersten Puppen ohne Führungsdrähte konnte man ansehen, daß sie sich die Gängelei ohnehin nicht mehr lange hätten gefallen lassen: Sie ähneln sehr den selbstbewußten, ja, beinahe frivolen Flapperpuppen der Zwanziger Jahre, wie Lotte Pritzel sie damals schuf. Eine davon kaufte Frau Lohrmann, die einen der ersten Puppenläden in Deutschland führte. Die Puppe war ein Flappergirl in einem roséfarbenen, harlekinähnlichen Hosenanzug mit Halskrause. Eines Tages, kurz danach, erhielt Hildegard Günzel einen Brief von Frau Lohrmann, zusammen mit einer Schallplatte der Firma Decca. Und siehe da! - sie traute ihren Augen nicht - auf dem Cover prangte ihre Flapperpuppe aus Cernit! Ein deutlicher Beweis dafür, daß die Puppenmacherin schon mit ihren ersten Schöpfungen den Zeitgeist getroffen hatte.

shades. They were stripped in caustic tanks to reveal their natural grain and they were decorated with objects, which were likewise purchased at the flea market or in antique shops. And this is how Hildegard Günzel's first encounter, or rather re-encounter, with dolls took place. One day, while visiting friends, she stood fascinated in front of an old pine cupboard with antique dolls, which at that time also suddenly popped up in flea markets. Admittedly the prices at the beginning of the seventies could not be compared to those of today, but they were nevertheless beyond the financial reach of young people in their mid-twenties. Other things were more important. The family came first. But Hildegard Günzel's „Childlike soul" (Günzel) felt as if it was being appealed to by the unusual creatures. They made something in her almost ring out. Almost forgotten emotions welled up from the depth of her unconscious. They remembered her of her childhood days when she pushed her dolls pram along the town wall of her romantic home town of Tauberbischofsheim. The desire grew in her to have a dolls collection too. But how could you - with no money?. But was she not an artist then? Had she not graduated from her design course with a degree? „Since I could not afford to buy myself any old dolls, I decided to make myself some". This was the impulse to be creative herself, and which started the ball rolling. The same thing had happened decades previously, also to another famous German dollmaker, Käthe Kruse, and years later Hildegard Günzel was to hear again and again of other ladies too, who make dolls. First of all however, Hildegard bought a pine cupboard. There still wasn't a doll which she could have put in it. But soon afterwards, there it was, the first Günzel doll ! It had a head made of plaster with large eyes and legs with cast-shaped shoes. The clothes were a problem. That was not because Hildegard Günzel couldn't make them, but because she didn't want to make them. Hildegard Günzel had always had an

Die größte Cernit-Puppe, die sie modellierte, war 1 m groß! Schwer sind Puppen aus Cernit immer, obwohl der Untergrund meist aus einer Styroporkugel besteht, über die die Knetmasse modelliert wird. Zuerst hatten deshalb alle Puppen gemalte Augen, später waren die Köpfe ausgehöhlt und hatten eingesetzte Glasaugen. In der Folge entstanden Dekorationspuppen, süße Puppen mit großen Augen und viel Spitze, die in einer Zeit, in der man sich durch zunehmende atomare Aufrüstung, steigende Kriminalität und Terrorismus ernsthaft bedroht fühlte, die Sehnsucht nach einer besseren, heileren Welt befriedigten. Noch immer existierte keine Sammlerszene, noch immer lag die Puppenwelt in tiefem Schlummer, doch zum ersten Mal nach langen Jahren der Abstinenz kauften Frauen wieder Puppen für sich selbst, nicht nur für ihre Kinder. Hildegard Günzel spürte diese unbewußte Sehnsucht der Frauen. Von Anfang an entwarf sie keine Spielpuppen für Kinder. Ihre Geschöpfe sind kleine, idealisierte Abbilder des Menschen, mitunter Charaktere, die man zu kennen glaubt, Gestalten aus Träumen oder flüchtige Erinnerungsbilder aus einer längst versunkenen Zeit.

Die Frauen waren begeistert - und faßten spontan denselben Entschluß wie einst Hildegard Günzel beim Betrachten der antiken Vorbilder: Sie wollten selbst Puppen modellieren. So gab die Puppenmacherin schon damals Puppenkurse mit Cernit. Ziemlich blauäugig, wie sie später zugab. „Eigentlich wußte ich damals nicht viel mehr als meine Kursusteilnehmer". Das tat der Freude indes keinen Abbruch. Denn um sie ging es dabei ja vordringlich. Damals stand das Kommerzielle noch nicht im Vordergrund. Niemand hätte sich damals träumen lassen, daß man mit Puppenmachen auch Geld verdienen kann. Hildegard Günzel gab eifrig Cernit- und Salzteigkurse und lernte so gleichzeitig mit ihren Teilnehmerinnen, „denn durch jeden Fehler lernt man mehr dazu, verbessert man seine eigenen Fähigkeiten. Man lernt durch Lehren".

aversion to sewing. Designing clothes, yes she does that with enthusiasm, since she just about revels in materials, lace and ribbons. But if at all possible somebody else ought to carry out her ideas. Today specialists are responsible for the wardrobe of the Günzel dolls. At that time, 1972, she still had to do everything herself. But the craving to see the completed doll before her very eyes also made this work easier. The search for perfect form began with the first doll. And associated with this was the search for the material best-suited for this purpose which allowed the ideas of the artist be implemented. In those days there were still no firms supplying dolls accessories. In those days if someone had admitted to making dolls he would have been met with astonishment from all sides. In the worst case one would have been laughed at. What! A grown-up woman fiddling around with those children's toys? Hildegard Günzel had been experimenting for about two years when the first block of cernite fell into her hands through the company for which she wrote instructions for handicrafts. The pliability of the material, its ease of use, and not least the wax-like lustre which objects made of cernite have, led to Hildegard Günzel's hobby developing into a profession. Gradually she discovered the manifold avenues which cernite opened up to her. The first of the dolls produced by her were pendants. They were small stylised figures of women with - shocking! - profiled breasts. They could be worn around the neck on a strip of leather. They went really well with Indian and hippie clothing, and they went just as well with jeans too, and in addition to this, they epitomised the feminine self-consciousness of the new modern woman, as propagated by the magazine „Emma", whose enthusiastic female readership included even Hildegard Günzel at that time. At some point in time the pendant became larger and heavier „until they could no longer be worn around the neck". Unwittingly they had been transformed into puppets. Did Hildegard Günzel

Cernitpuppe 1974
Cernit doll 1974.

think that she could keep her passion for dolls under control more easily as long as she had them on a string? Perhaps. But in the end she did let them off the leash. You could see from the first dolls which weren't controlled on the end of a length of string that they wouldn't have liked being kept on a string for much longer anyway. They very much resemble the self-conscious, indeed, almost frivolous flapper dolls of the twenties, such as the ones created by Lotte Pritzel in that era. One of them was purchased by Mrs Lohrmann, who ran one of the first dolls' emporiums in Germany. The doll was a flapper in a pink-coloured harlequin-like trouser suit with a ruff. One day, shortly afterwards, Hildegard Günzel received a letter from Mrs Lohrmann together with a record manufactured by Decca. And lo and behold - she couldn't believe her eyes - on the cover was displayed her flapper doll made of cernite. A clear indication that Hildegard Günzel had tapped into the spirit of the age with her very first creation. The largest cernite - doll which she modelled was 1 metre tall! Dolls made of cernite are inevitably heavy, although the base material mostly consists of styro foam pellets, on top of which is the modelling material. For this reason all the dolls initially had eyes painted on, but later on the heads were recessed and had glass eyes inserted. As a result decorative dolls were created, sweet dolls with large eyes and lots of lace, which satisfied the longing for a better, more intact world in an age in which people felt seriously threatened by an escalation in the stockpiling of atomic weapons, and the rising tide of criminality and terrorism. There still wasn't a collectors' scene, the world of dolls was still in deep slumber, but for the first time after many years of abstinence, women were buying dolls not only for their children, but also for themselves again. Hildegard Günzel felt this unconscious longing of women. From the beginning she had not designed dolls for children to play with. Her creations are small idealised replicas of people, occasionally cha-

Die Kursusteilnehmer waren und sind bis heute zum größten Teil Frauen, für die die Puppenkurse nicht nur Gelegenheiten waren, sich für ein paar Stunden oder Tage ganz ihrem Hobby zu widmen. Darüber hinaus waren es reizende gesellschaftliche Anlässe. Man traf sich in netter Runde, plauderte miteinander, sprach mitunter auch über Probleme, und nach und nach entwickelte sich ein für viele der Frauen damals neues Gefühl von Solidarität. Manch eine Kursusteilnehmerin wurde dadurch selbstbewußter. Nach dem Kursus ging man gemeinsam essen, und es wurde von Mal zu Mal später. Am Anfang, erzählte Hildegard Günzel, sprachen die Frauen meistens (begeistert und des Lobes voll) über ihre Männer und Kinder. Bald wurden jedoch andere Töne angeschlagen: Je mehr die Frauen ihrem neuen Steckenpferd frönten, desto häufiger beklagten sich ihre Männer: über herumliegende Stoffe, Farben, Pinsel usw. - und über das neue Selbstwertgefühl ihrer Frauen, die über derartige männliche Querelen in der Zwischenzeit erhaben waren und sie ungerührt über sich ergehen ließen. Nur in den Kursen, unter „Leidens"gefährtinnen, machte sich ihre Empörung über das männliche Unverständnis Luft. „Nach 12 Kursustagen waren alle total emanzipiert" (Günzel). „Besonders wohlriechend" waren die Kurse allerdings dann, wenn sich ein mutiger Mann unter den Teilnehmern befand. Dann „wurden alle Frauen besonders liebenswürdig. Sie kamen in hübschen Kleidern und benutzten Parfum. Ein Mann im Kursus wertete ihn offensichtlich auf, verlieh ihm etwas Wichtiges. Plötzlich war Puppenmachen ein ernst zu nehmendes Hobby geworden". Einer der Männer, die es wagten, in diese Frauen-Domäne einzubrechen, war Lothar Größle. Hildegard Günzel: „Lothar Größle ist sehr begabt. Eigentlich brauchte er keinen Kursus, er wollte nur eine ganz bestimmte Technik erlernen, um sie dann als Lehrer im Unterricht weitergeben zu können". Eine nette Puppenfreundschaft entwickelte sich zwischen ihnen. Die Puppende-

racters, whom one thinks one knows, figures from dreams or fleeting images of memories of an age long past. The women were enthusiastic - and spontaneously made the same decision as Hildegard Günzel had once done when looking at the antique models; they wanted to model dolls themselves. So even then Hildegard Günzel gave courses in doll making with cernite. Fairly green behind the ears, as she was later to admit. „Actually at that time I didn't know much more than the people on my courses." But that didn't detract from the pleasure she derived from it. For they were indeed her priority. At that stage the commercial aspect was not yet in the foreground. No-one then would have dreamed that it is even possible to earn money with doll making. Hildegard Günzel gave cernite and salt-dough courses enthusiastically, and by doing so learned at the same time as her course participants. „Because with every mistake you make, you learn, and improve your own skills. You learn by teaching." The course participants were, and to this day still are, for the most part ladies for whom the dolls' courses were not only an opportunity to devote themselves entirely to their hobby for a few hours or days. In addition to this there were charming social reasons. You could meet up in pleasant company, chat with one another, occasionally discuss problems, and gradually a new feeling of solidarity developed at that time for many of the women. Many a course participant gained in self-consciousness. At the end of the courses the participants went out for a meal together and on each occasion these meals lasted longer and longer. At the beginning, recounted Hildegard Günzel, the women mostly spoke (with enthusiasm and with praise) about their husbands and children. However they soon changed their tune. The more the women became addicted to their new hobby, the more frequently their men complained about materials left lying around, paints, brushes etc., and about the new sense of self-worth of their wives, who in

6 Jahre liegen zwischen diesen beiden Puppen.
(rechts 1979, links 1985)

*These two dolls are separated by 6 years
(right 1979, left 1985).*

signerin mietete ihr 1. „Puppenhaus" in El-
cheshain-Illingen von Lothar Größle.
Dem Cernit ist sie lange Zeit treu geblieben.
Noch 1984, als sie schon längst zu Porzellan
übergegangen war, modellierte sie alle Modell-
köpfe zuerst aus Cernit.
Ein paar Jahre gingen ins Land, in denen Hildegard Günzel ihre Puppen auf kleineren Ausstellungen in Karlsruhe und Umgebung prä-

the meanwhile were above such petty male
squabbling and patiently suffered this without
taking it to heart. Only in the courses amongst their „fellow sufferers" did they give vent
to the male lack of understanding. „After 12
days on the course all the participants were
totally emancipated" (Günzel). Mind you, the
courses were 'particularly fragrant' when there
was a brave man amongst the participants.

Lydia Gehrig, Hildegard Günzel´s Mutter mit der ersten Porzellanpuppe, die zu ihrer Sammlung gehört.

Lydia Gehrig, Hildegard Günzel's mother with the first porcelain doll in her collection.

sentierte. Dann, Ende der siebziger Jahre, „ es ist schwer, sich an alle diese Daten exakt zu erinnern, ich wußte damals ja nicht, daß das einmal wichtig werden könnte" (Günzel) , auf dem Handwerkermarkt in Karlsruhe, sprach sie eine Dame an. Wie sich herausstellte, kam sie vom Kaufhaus Beck in München. Sie fragte die junge Puppenkünstlerin, ob sie nicht Lust hätte, ihre Puppen im „Weihnachtshaus" des Kaufhauses auszustellen. Wieder einmal sollte von einem Münchner Kaufhaus der Anfang der Künstlerpuppenszene in Deutschland ausgehen. Hildegard Günzel sagte für das nächste Mal zu. Doch zuvor fand ihre erste Ausstellung 1980 im „Blauen Haus" statt. Das „Blaue Haus" in Karlsruhe ist eine Galerie, die immer noch besteht.

Durch Bekannte hatte sie die Inhaber, ein Architektenehepaar, kennengelernt, das in dem Haus mit seiner interessanten Architektur monatliche, exklusive Ausstellungen mit unterschiedlicher Thematik veranstaltete, die von einem sehr guten Publikum besucht wurden. Hildegard Günzels Puppen und Marionetten wurden zusammen mit exquisitem Schmuck, Bildern und Gläsern präsentiert. „Diese Ausstellung war damals das Eleganteste, was ich gemacht habe".

Doch in diesem Jahr trat die entscheidende Wende in ihrem Werk ein: Sie entdeckte das Porzellan als Werkstoff. Noch ergab sie sich dem neuen Material nicht ganz und gar. Die Modelle entstanden zunächst aus Cernit und wurden anschließend in Porzellan ausgeführt. Doch Hildegard Günzel vermißte den wachsartigen Schimmer, den Cernitpuppen besitzen, und der der Hautfarbe der Puppen jenen „lebendigen" Hauch verleiht, der Betrachter den Atem anhalten läßt, weil sie glauben, die Puppen müßten sich gleich zu bewegen anfangen. So ging sie dazu über, das Biskuit nach der Bemalung mit einer hauchzarten Wachsschicht zu überziehen.

Heute bevorzugen die meisten Puppenmacher das Porzellan. Warum? Gibt es dafür tiefer lie-

Then „All the women were especially kind". They turned up in pretty dresses and wore perfume. A man on the course evidently upgraded it, and imparted it a sense of importance. Suddenly doll-making had become a hobby to be taken seriously". One of the men who dared to break into this female domain was Lothar Größle, Hildegard Günzel says the following about him, „Lothar Größle is very talented. Actually he didn't need to come on a course, he only wanted to learn one very specific technique, in order to be able to teach it himself in his classes." A pleasant friendship developed between them revolving around dolls. Hildegard Günzel rented her first „House of Dolls" in Elcheshain - Illingen from Lothar Größle. She has remained faithful to cernite for a long time. Even in 1984 when she had already gone over to porcelain for a long time, she initially modelled all heads from cernite. A few years passed during which time Hildegard Günzel showed her dolls at smaller exhibitions in Karlsruhe and the surrounding area. Then, at the end of the 1970s, („It is difficult to give precise dates for all these events, I certainly didn't know at that time that they could become important" (Günzel)) at the craft market in Karlsruhe, a lady spoke to Hildegard Günzel. As it turned out, she had come from the Beck department store in Munich. She asked the young doll artist whether she wouldn't like to exhibit her dolls in the „Christmas section" of the department store. Once again the beginning of the artistic doll scene in Germany was to take off from a department store in Munich. Hildegard Günzel agreed to exhibit on the following occasion. But prior to that her first exhibition took place in the 'Blue House' in 1980. The 'Blue House' in Karlsruhe is a gallery which is still in existence. Hildegard Günzel had got to know the owners, an architect - couple through acquaintances. They staged exclusive monthly exhibitions on various subjects in the house which boasted interesting architectural features. These exhibitions were very well

gende Gründe? Es hat vielleicht doch nicht nur mit den Puppen des 19. Jahrhunderts zu tun, mit denen in unseren Tagen die Sammelleidenschaft begann. Ob es nicht vielmehr das Material selbst ist, das die Künstler begeistert? Porzellan, das „weiße Gold", war der modernste Werkstoff zur Zeit des Rokoko und der frühen Klassik. Das war das Zeitalter der verfeinerten Sitten, der Hochblüte der Kunst, und zwar der bildenden wie der Musik. Es war die Epoche Mozarts und Goethes. Lord Byron wurde damals geboren. Doch das ausgehende 18. Jahrhundert kennzeichnete auch der Übergang von der alten Weltordnung zur neuen. Das Chaos regierte im revolutionären Frankreich. Die Staaten der USA schüttelten das englische Joch ab. Es war die Zeit der Befreiung des Geistes, der Emanzipation der Unterdrückten. Ist es also ein Wunder, daß emanzipierte Frauen Porzellanpuppen machen? Doch Revolten stören die Harmonie. Künstler denken nicht politisch. Die Menschen des beginnenden 19. Jahrhunderts zogen sich zurück auf innere Werte. Es war auch die Zeit der Wiederentdeckung der Empfindsamkeit, eine Zeit, die wir „Romantik" nennen. Ist es ein Wunder, daß unsere Puppenkünstler heute ähnlich empfinden? In einer Zeit, in der vielerorts das Chaos herrscht, sich zurückziehen auf eine innere, „heilere" Welt? Empfindsamkeit zulassen und sie in ihren Geschöpfen sichtbar machen in einer Epoche der grausamsten Kriege der Menschheitsgeschichte? Es wäre nur natürlich. Und zu begrüßen.

Doch zurück zum Anfang der 80er Jahre unseres Jahrhunderts, nach München, ins Kaufhaus Beck: Mit Herzklopfen brachte Hildegard Günzel ihre neuen und „alten" Puppen - aus Cernit und Porzellan - zur Weihnachtsausstellung nach München. Merkwürdig und befremdlich erschien es ihr, daß ihre Porzellanpuppen von den Verantwortlichen nicht mit der spontanen Begeisterung aufgenommen wurden, die sie eigentlich erwartet hatte. Dann erkannte sie den Grund: Sie war nicht

1. Preis, Wettbewerb der Global Doll Society, 1983.
First prize at the Global Doll Society competition in 1983.

attended. Hildegard Günzel's dolls and puppets were presented together with exquisite jewellery, pictures and glasses. 'At that time this exhibition was the most elegant thing I had ever done' (Günzel). But it was in the same year that the decisive turning point came in Hildegard Günzel's work; she discovered porcelain as a material. She still didn't commit herself completely to the new material. Initially the models were created with cernite and following that they were finished with porcelain. But Hildegard Günzel missed the wax-like sheen which cernite dolls have, and which imparts that 'living' tinge to the skin colour of the dolls, which makes onlookers hold their breath because they think that the doll is about to move. And so she went over to covering the bisque after painting with a wafer-thin layer of wax. Nowadays most doll makers prefer porcelain. Why? Are there deeper reasons for this? It is perhaps not only to do with the dolls of the nineteenth century with which the passion for collecting began in our era. Whether it isn't rather the material itself which inspires the artists. Porcelain the 'white gold' was the most modern material of

die einzige Puppenmacherin mit dieser Technik auf der Welt. Brigitte Deval war schon vor ihr dagewesen, sie stellte bereits seit 1978 im „Beck" ihre wachsüberzogenen Porzellanpuppen aus. Brigitte Deval war damals schon ein Profi und mit dem Werkstoff Porzellan seit langem vertraut. Neben ihr kam sie sich zunächst wie ein Neuling vor. Sie war „wie erschlagen, denn ich wußte gar nicht, daß es außer mir noch andere Puppenmacherinnen gab". Den in der Frauenzeitschrift „Brigitte" erschienenen Artikel über Brigitte Deval hatte sie - als passionierte „Emma"-Leserin - „natürlich nicht gelesen". Dieses Verhalten ist normal, denn, wie J.W. von Goethe, Deutschlands größter Dichter, einmal so treffend

1. Preis, Wettbewerb der Global Doll Society, 1984 (Aschenputtel).
First prize at the Global Doll Society competition in 1984 (Aschenputtel).

the rococo era and early classicism. That was the age of refined manners, the zenith of art, and to be more precise of the visual arts as well as music. It was the epoch of Mozart and Goethe. Lord Byron was born at that time. But the close of the eighteenth century also marked the transition from the old to the new world order. Chaos ruled in revolutionary France. The United States shook off the English yoke. It was the epoch of the liberation of the spirit, the emancipation of the oppressed. Is it therefore any wonder, that emancipated ladies make porcelain dolls? But revolts upset harmony. Artists are not political. At the beginning of the nineteenth century people withdrew to inner values. It was also the era of the rediscovery of sensitivity, an era which we call the 'Romantic era'. Is it any wonder that our doll artists have similar emotions today. Withdrawing to an inner, more intact world in an age in which chaos rules in many places. Admitting sensitivity and making it visible in their creations in an epoch of the most inhuman wars in the history of mankind. This is only natural. And this is to be welcomed. But let us return to the beginning of the 1980s to the Beck department store in Munich. Her heart was beating as Hildegard Günzel brought her new and „old" dolls - made of cernite and porcelain - to the Christmas exhibition in Munich. It seemed strange and surprising to her that her porcelain dolls were not received with spontaneous enthusiasm from those persons in positions of responsibility, as she had actually expected. Then she found out the reason. She was not the only lady doll-maker in the world using this technique. Brigitte Deval had already been practising it before her, and had already been exhibiting her wax-coated porcelain dolls in the „Beck" department store since 1978. Brigitte Deval was already a professional at that time and had been familiar with porcelain as a material for a long time. Next to her Hildegard Günzel at first felt like a newcomer. She was „…stunned, since I was-

bemerkte: „Zu erfinden, zu beschließen, bleibt der Künstler stets allein. Seine Arbeit zu genießen eilt er freudig zum Verein". Zwar gab es damals schon Puppenkünstlerinnen, doch sie blieben für sich. Jede probierte, experimentierte, werkelte für sich allein. Es ist das große, bisher noch nicht recht gewürdigte Verdienst des Kaufhauses Beck, diesen Umstand geändert und die Basis geschaffen zu haben, daß Deutschlands Puppenkünstlerinnen voneinander erfuhren und - voneinander lernten. Das „Beck" hat damit maßgeblich zu der Entwicklung der Szene in Deutschland beigetragen. Hildegard Günzel erzählt freimütig, daß sie sich von Devals Arbeit anspornen ließ, denn „sie war schon weiter. Ihre Puppen faszinierten mich, sie übten einen eigenartigen Reiz auf mich aus". Später schrieb sie diesen Reiz unter anderem der Tatsache zu, daß Brigitte Deval in Italien lebt und sich von den klassischen Frauengestalten der Renaissance und Antike inspirieren ließ.

Bei der Ausstellung ein Jahr später sahen die Günzel-Puppen ganz anders aus. „Sie waren mehr ich, mehr Menschlein" (Günzel). Sie hatte den Schritt endgültig vollzogen: weg von der niedlichen Dekorationspuppe, hin zu einer naturalistisch-idealistischen Darstellung des Menschen, der sie von nun an treu bleiben und die sie immer mehr vervollkommnen würde. Dieses Mal war die Konkurrenz noch größer: Rotraut Schrott, Annette Himstedt und Ingrid Tilmann kamen dazu. Annette Himstedt gestand ihr später, daß sie beim Anblick der Günzel-Puppen denselben Schock erlebt hatte wie Hildegard Günzel ein Jahr zuvor. Auch sie hatte geglaubt, die einzige Puppenmacherin weit und breit zu sein. Nach und nach fanden sich immer mehr Puppenkünstlerinnen im Kaufhaus Beck zur Weihnachtszeit ein. Und schließlich war dort „die geballte Puppenwelt vertreten. - Ich wollte mehr Luft haben" (Günzel). Mehr Raum sollte sie bekommen, „mehr Luft" nicht. Sie traf Matthias Wanke, und in den Folgemonaten begann eine geradezu atemberaubende Karriere.

n't even aware that there were any other dollmakers besides myself". Since, as an enthusiastic reader of „Emma" she hadn't read of course about the article on Brigitte Deval which appeared in the women's magazine „Brigitte". This behaviour is normal since, as J. W. von Goethe, Germany's greatest poet and writer once remarked so aptly,

„To delve, to resolve, the artist on his very own must always be.
To savour his labours, in brisk bonhomie to his club must he."

Admittedly there were lady doll-makers even then, but they kept to themselves. Each one of them was trying out techniques, experimenting, pottering around on their own. It is thanks to the „Beck" department store, and to date this service still hasn't been properly recognised, that these circumstances have been changed and have created an environment in which Germany's lady doll-makers have been able to learn about and from one another. In so doing the „Beck" department store has made a decisive contribution to the scene in Germany. Hildegard Günzel relates candidly that she was spurred on by Deval's work, for, „She was already ahead of me. Her dolls fascinated me, they exerted a unique charm on me"! Later she ascribed this charm, amongst other things, to the fact that Brigitte Deval lives in Italy and was inspired by the classical women's figures of the renaissance and antiquity. At the exhibition, a year later the Günzel dolls looked quite different. 'They were no longer me, but rather little people' (Günzel). At last she had taken the step away from the dainty decorative doll over to a natural-idealised representation of people, to whom she would remain faithful from now on, and whom she would improve again and again. This time the competition was even greater. Rotraut Schrott, Annette Himstedt, and Ingrid Tilmann had been added. Annette Himstedt later admitted to her that when she looked at the Günzel dolls she had experienced the same shock as Hildegard Günzel had

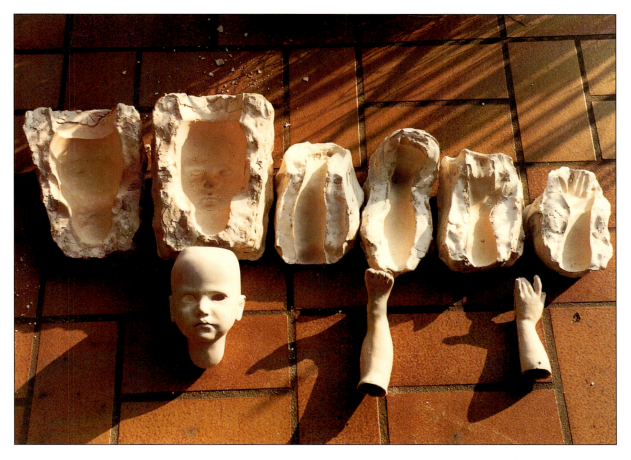

Die ersten Gipsformen, hier Georgina. „Es ist noch
kein Meister vom Himmel gefallen."
The first plaster figures, here Georgina. „No one was born
master of a trade".

experienced a year previously. She too had
thought that she was the only lady doll-maker
far and wide. Gradually more and more lady
doll-makers turned up at the „Beck" department store at Christmas time. And in the end
the whole caboodle of the doll's world showed
up. I wanted more space (Günzel). She was to
have more room, but not more space. She met
Matthias Wanke and in the following months
her virtually breathtaking and staggering
career took off.

Georgina, die erste Puppe, die 1984 für eine Reproduktionsform freigegeben wurde, 1985, eine der erfolgreichsten Formen auf der Welt.

Georgina, the first doll which was to be released for reproduction in 1984 was one of the most successful mold in the world in 1985.

Puppenträume ganz in Weiß. 1980 - 1985
Dolls' dreams all in white 1980 - 1985

Matthias Wanke war eine schillernde Persönlichkeit der Puppenszene. Ein gutaussehender junger Mann mit langen, dunklen Locken, einem Schnurrbart, kessen Cowboystiefeln und engen Hosen. In seiner „Puppenfamilie", die ja überwiegend aus Frauen bestand, die meistens viel älter waren als er, war er „Hahn im Korb"- und durchaus in der Lage, Aufruhr in weiblichen Herzen zu verursachen. Darüber hinaus war er ein weitblickender Geschäftsmann.

Bereits als Schüler von 18 Jahren trödelte Matthias Wanke auf Frankfurter Flohmärkten. Dabei fiel ihm das stetig wachsende Interesse an antiken Puppen und Ersatzteilen auf. Er begann, sich umfassend über dieses anscheinend neue Sammelgebiet zu informieren. So erfuhr er, daß das Zentrum der ehemaligen deutschen Puppenproduktion in Thüringen war. Ende der siebziger Jahre lag Thüringen noch auf dem Gebiet der damaligen DDR. Matthias Wanke fuhr also in die DDR und schaffte es, dort Kontakte zu ehemaligen Puppenherstellern und Museen zu knüpfen. Er lernte viel über die alten Herstellungsmethoden und brachte wundervolle antike Puppen, den Grundstock der (augenblicklich im Museum der Stadt Ratingen untergebrachten) Sammlung Wanke, von dort mit nach Hause. Als gerade Zwanzigjähriger, 1977, gründete er eine eigene Firma und war auf Messen vertreten. Zu seinem Angebot gehörten von Anfang an Puppen. Die ersten waren preiswerte Artikel aus Asien, die über Geschenkartikelläden vertrieben wurden. Doch Matthias Wanke war von den antiken Puppen fasziniert. Warum sollte man die alten Herstellungstechniken eigentlich nicht wiederbeleben? In seiner Firma in Limburg/Taunus setzte er diese Idee aus den USA kurzerhand in die Tat um. In Seminaren wurden Reproduktionspuppen nach alten Modellen gefertigt. In den angelsächsi-

Matthias Wanke was a dazzling personality on the doll scene. A good-looking young man with long, dark locks, a moustache, jaunty cowboy boots and tight trousers. He was the „cock of the walk" amongst his 'doll family' which indeed mostly consisted of ladies who were mostly much older than him, and he was certainly in a position to make female hearts flutter. In addition to this he was a far-sighted businessman. Even as an 18 year old sixth-former, Matthias Wanke was dawdling around the flea markets in Frankfurt. As he did so, he noticed the continually growing interest in antique dolls and spare parts. He began to acquire a comprehensive knowledge of this apparently new sphere of interest for collectors. This is how he discovered that the centre of the former doll manufacturing area in Germany was in Thüringia, which in the late 1970s was still part of the former East Germany (GDR). Matthias Wanke consequently went to East Germany in order to establish contact with former doll-manufacturers and museums. He learned a great deal about the old methods of manufacture and brought wonderful antique dolls, which were to form the basis of the Wanke collection (presently housed in the Ratingen Town museum), back home from Thüringia. Just twenty years old in 1977, he founded his own company and went to trade fairs. Dolls were part of his range from the start. The first ones were good-value articles from Asia, which were sold via giftware shops. But Matthias Wanke was fascinated by antique dolls. Why shouldn't the old manufacturing techniques actually be resurrected? He implemented this idea from the USA without hesitation in his company in Limburg in the Taunus region. Reproduction dolls were produced to look like old models in seminars. At that time doll-making was already a widespread hobby in the Anglo-Saxon

Froschkönig, 1986.
The princess with the frog , 1986.

Aschenputtel, 1985.
Aschenputtel, 1985.
Doty Award
Doll Reader Magazin,
USA

25

Hänsel und Gretel, 1985.
Hansel and Gretel, 1985.

schen Ländern und vor allem in den USA war Puppenmachen damals schon ein verbreiteteres Hobby. Er gewann Carol Ann Stanton, Ginny Regopoulos und Debbie Stanton als Mitarbeiter und Seminarleiter. „Der Puppenbrief", als dessen Herausgeber Carol Ann Stanton, Ginny Regopoulos, Matthias Wanke und Debbie Stanton fungierten, wurde erstmalig im November 1981 in einer Auflage von 10.000 Stück an alte und potentielle Neukunden und Puppeninteressierte versandt. Es hieß dort in der Anrede: „Liebe Freunde! Willkommen zum ersten „Puppen-Brief". Dieser wird Ihnen gratis zugesandt, um eine weltweite Freundschaft der Puppensammler und -Hersteller zu fördern. Wir hoffen, damit die Puppenfanatiker dieser Welt in Verbindung zu halten...". Auf Seite 4 wurde über die ersten in Limburg abgehaltenen Seminare berichtet: „Spezialreportage. Limburger Puppenherstellungs-Seminare. 14 und 15., 17. und 18., 20. und 21. Oktober 1981. Studenten aus Deutschland, der Schweiz, England und Frankreich kamen nach Limburg, um an den von Matthias Wanke zusammengestellten Seminaren teilzunehmen. Diese Veranstaltung war in Europa einmalig. Ein solcher Kurs hat außerhalb der USA noch nie stattgefunden...". Fertiggestellt wurden in diesen ersten Seminaren Europas: die Charakterpuppe Serien-Nr. 114 von Kämmer & Reinhardt (Anfänger) und eine Jumeau mit geschlossenem Mund (Fortgeschrittene!). Die Ära der freiwilligen Klausur der Puppenkünstlerinnen war damit vorbei. Ein neues Zeitalter war angebrochen: das der „weltweiten Freundschaft durch Puppen".

Im Herbst 1977 hatte der erste „Puppenkongreß" Deutschlands in Tecklenburg stattgefunden. Dieser ersten Börse folgten rasch weitere: in Frankfurt, Hamburg, München, Düsseldorf usw. Bei einer solchen Gelegenheit traf Hildegard Günzel eines Tages Matthias Wanke und fragte ihn, ob sie auf einer seiner Börsen ausstellen könnte. Sie bekam einen Tisch „und war völlig versteckt zwischen antiken

countries, above all in the USA. He gained Carol Ann Stanton, Ginny Regopoulos, and Debbie Stanton, as staff and seminar leaders. A print run of 10,000 copies of „Der Puppenbrief", for whom Carol Ann Stanton, Giny Regopoulos, Matthias Wanke, and Debbie Stanton acted as editors, was sent out for the first time in November 1981 to old and potential new customers and those interested in dolls. In the salutation it said „Dear Friends! Welcome to the first edition of „Puppenbrief". This has been sent to you free of charge, in support of the world-wide „friendship of doll-collectors and makers. We hope to keep all the doll fanatics of the world in contact with this". On page 4 there was a report about the first seminars held in Limburg; „Special reports. Limburg dollmaking seminars 14th and 15th, 17th and 18th, 20th and 21st October, 1981. Students came to Limburg to take part in the seminars put together by Matthias Wanke from Germany, Switzerland, England, and France. This event was unique in Europe. There had never been such a course held outside the USA before". In these first European seminars were produced the character dolls series no. 114 Von Kämmer & Reinhardt (for beginners) and a Jumeau with a closed mouth (for advanced students !). The era of voluntary meetings given by lady doll-artists was therefore over. A new age had dawned, that of „world-wide friendship through dolls". The first „Dolls congress" in Germany had taken place in Tecklenburg in Autumn 1977. This first dolls' exchange was followed rapidly by others in Frankfurt, Hamburg, Munich, Düsseldorf etc. It was at just such an occasion that Hildegard Günzel met Matthias Wanke and asked him whether she could exhibit at one of his exchanges. She was given a table and was completely tucked away between antique dolls. In the early years exchanges were primarily sales shows for antique dealers. Amongst them however were also scattered stands with reproduction artists, who were

Matthias Wanke, Mitbegründer der Global Doll
Society, erster Geschäftspartner im Puppengeschäft.
*Matthias Wanke, co-founder of the Global Doll Society,
Hildegard Günzel's first business-partner in the doll
business.*

Puppen". Börsen waren in den Anfangsjahren
in erster Linie Verkaufsschauen von An-
tikhändlern. Dazwischen fanden sich verein-
zelt jedoch auch schon Stände von Reproduk-
tionskünstlern, die von den Antiksammlern
meistens scheel von der Seite betrachtet wurden, denn man sah in diesen eine Gefahr für
den Antikmarkt. Künstlerpuppen waren damals noch etwas ganz Neues, nie Dagewese-
nes. Mit Staunen, Bewunderung und auch mit
Befremden wurden die neuartigen Puppen,
die so ganz anders aussahen als die gewohnten,
betrachtet. Auf die häufig gestellte Frage der
Besucher, von wann die Puppen seien, antwortete Hildegard Günzel immer: „Von ge-
stern" oder „von heute". Häufig kritisierten

mostly given sidelong, grudging glances from
the antique collectors, since they were regar-
ded as a threat to the antique market. Artistic
dolls were at that time still something very
new, never beholden by human eyes. The new
type of doll, which looked quite different
from the accustomed ones, were looked at
with astonishment, amazement, and even
indignation. To the question frequently asked
by visitors as to which the era the dolls belonged, Hildegard Günzel always replied, 'From
yesterday' or 'From today'. Often the visitors
criticised the hands and feet, which in their
opinion, had turned out too large. Hildegard
Günzel then patiently expounded the theory
of anatomy and proportion every time and in
this way gave many a visitor a more critical eye
for her enchanting doll-creations. In order to
make the differentness of her dolls clear and
also to keep them distinct from the up-and-
coming competition, Hildegard Günzel
thought up a marketing strategy. For example
she forewent having business cards printed
and in response to being asked her name
always responded with „Günzel". This is how
her name eventually sank in. Matthias Wanke
gave her the same table in every exchange.
Hildegard always covered it with a white cloth
and dressed all her dolls in white or cream, so
that „Everyone saw my table immediately as
they came in". Her tender, elf-like or angelic
children with their translucent skin really did
enchant the world of dolls at that time. These
early Günzel dolls never had shoes, so that the
beautiful modelling of their feet could be
seen. As a result they looked guileless and vul-
nerable, tranquil and soft - with their dreamy
blue eyes, innocent and fragile. And many of
the inveterate antique collectors suddenly had
a new hobby after their first encounter with
Günzel dolls - collecting artistic dolls ! In
those days Hildegard Günzel exhibited her
dolls in galleries in southern Germany, but
also even in Paris, Switzerland, and in the
Netherlands. The foundation of the Wanke
Company and its product range was of great

die Besucher die ihrer Meinung nach zu groß geratenen Hände und Füße. Die Künstlerin erläuterte dann jedes Mal geduldig Anatomie- und Proportionslehre und schärfte auf diese Weise bei manch einem Betrachter den Blick für ihre zauberhaften Puppenkreationen. Um die Andersartigkeit ihrer Puppen deutlich zu machen und auch, um sich gegen die aufkommende Konkurrenz abzugrenzen, dachte sich Hildegard Günzel eine Marketing-Strategie aus. Sie verzichtete zum Beispiel darauf, Visitenkarten drucken zu lassen und antwortete auf die Frage nach ihrem Namen immer mit „Günzel". So prägte sich der Name schließlich ein. Matthias Wanke gab ihr an jedem Ort den gleichen Tisch. Hildegard Günzel bedeckte ihn immer mit einem weißen Tuch und zog alle ihre Puppen in Weiß oder Creme an, so daß „jeder meinen weißen Tisch sofort beim Hereinkommen sah". Ihre zarten, elfen- oder engelhaften Kinder mit ihrer durchscheinenden Haut bezauberten damals schon die Puppenwelt. Diese frühen Günzel-Puppen hatten nie Schuhe, damit man die schöne Modellierung ihrer Füße sehen konnte. Sie wirkten dadurch arglos und verletzlich, still und sanft - mit ihren verträumten blauen Augen, unschuldig und zerbrechlich. Und manch eine der eingefleischten Antiksammlerinnen hatte nach der ersten Begegnung mit Günzel-Puppen plötzlich ein neues Hobby: Künstlerpuppensammeln!

Die Designerin stellte damals in Galerien Süddeutschlands, doch auch schon in Paris, der Schweiz und denNiederlanden ihre Puppen aus.

Die Gründung der Firma Wanke und deren Sortiment waren für alle Puppenmacherinnen, eine große Hilfe. „Endlich brauchte man nicht mehr z. B. Perücken selber zu machen". Immer mehr Frauen - und zunehmend auch Männer - entdeckten Puppenmachen als befriedigendes und, in steigendem Maße, auch lukratives Hobby. Die Firma Wanke expandierte immer mehr. Von Anfang an war der „Puppen-Brief" zweisprachig. Schon in der

assistance to all lady doll makers, not only Hildegard Günzel. „At last one didn't need, for example, to make wigs oneself". More and more women - and increasingly men too - were discovering doll-making as a satisfying and in increasing measure, also as a lucrative hobby. The Wanke company expanded continually. From the beginning the „Puppen Brief" was bi-lingual. Even in the second edition from February 1982 could be read in English „AUSTRALIA!!! We like to export our products to Australia"!!! Below this were listed the individual articles: German papier mâché bodies, baby bodies, mouth-blown glass eyes etc. but the Wanke company still did not have any artistic dolls in its range. This state of affairs changed two years later. In the September edition in 1982, the „Global Doll Society" was announced on the penultimate page. „Global friendship through collecting dolls. A non-profit making global society for every doll-lover". One line beneath this was raised the question „Why should you become a member of the GLOBAL DOLL SOCIETY?" This was followed by ten arguments in favour of doing so, listed individually. Number 8 was, „Only members will be allowed to take part in G.D.S. doll competitions". The first competition of the newly founded „Global Doll Society" took place on the 2nd of October 1983 in Frankfurt. It was organised as part of the „Global Doll Congress" from 30th September until the 2nd October 1983 in Limburg. Participants registered from England, USA, Germany, Switzerland, France, the Netherlands, Spain, Belgium, Austria, Australia, Ireland, South Africa, Canada and Sweden. On the first day there was a sightseeing-tour on a steamer along the Rhine, on the second day there was a number of different workshops to visit.

Gruppe für die Ausstellung „Magischer Zirkus" in München, 1986.
Group for the "Magic Circus" exhibition in Munich, 1986.

Zum ersten Mal als Jurymitglied beim Wettbewerb der Global Doll Society. V.l. Debbie Stanton, Carol Ann Stanton, Ella Haas, die ihren Preis aus den Händen von Astry Campbell entgegen nimmt, Hildegard Günzel, Matthias Wanke.

As a member of the jury for the first time at the Global Doll Society competition. From left, Debbie Stanton, Carol Ann Stanton, Ella Haas receiving her prize from Astry Campbell, Hildegard Günzel, Matthias Wanke.

zweiten Ausgabe vom Februar 1982 konnte man auf Seite 9 in englischer Sprache lesen: „AUSTRALIA!!! We like to export our products to Australia!!!" Darunter wurden die einzelnen Artikel aufgeführt: deutsche Papiermachékörper, Babykörper, mundgeblasene Glasaugen usw. , doch noch keine Künstlerpuppe war im Sortiment der Firma Wanke vertreten. Das änderte sich zwei Jahre darauf.

In der September-Ausgabe 1982 wurde auf der vorletzten Seite die „Global Doll Society" angekündigt: „Weltweite Freundschaft durch Pupensammeln. Eine gemeinnützige, weltweite Gesellschaft für jeden Puppenliebhaber." Eine Zeile darunter wurde die Frage aufgeworfen: „Warum sollten Sie Mitglied der GLOBAL DOLL SOCIETY werden?" Im Anschluß daran wurden zehn Argumente, die dafür sprechen, einzeln aufgeführt. Nr. 8 hieß:

Amongst other things, Guiseppe Garella from Italy gave a lecture on the history of the Lenci dolls, François Theima gave one about French dolls, Ingrid Scheinhard gave one about antique dolls houses and dolls from dolls' houses. Carol Ann Stanton reported about collectable teddy-bears (which still are her passion, as you have yet to discover). Jackie Jacobs about antique dolls clothing and accessories, Simone Monville and Margaret Glover gave a lecture about restoring antique dolls and Laura Shreeve demonstrated how to knit wigs. Astry Campbell read a paper on American artistic dolls. On the third day of the convention, the 2nd of October 1983, in addition to the „1st doll competition in Europe the (in the meantime VIIIth) Frankfurt doll exchange was held too, in the „Frankfurter Hof" hotel. More than 80 exhi-

Nominierte Puppen für den Doty Award des Doll Reader Magazin werden im US-Fernsehen vorgestellt, durch den ehemaligen Verleger Garry Rudell.

Dolls nominated for Doty Awards by the Doll Reader Magazine are shown on TV in the USA by the former publisher Garry Rudell.

„Nur Mitgliedern wird die Teilnahme an G.D.S.-Puppenwettbewerben ermöglicht".

Der erste Wettbewerb der neu gegründeten „Global Doll Society" fand am 2. Oktober 1983 in Frankfurt statt.

Ausgerichtet wurde er im Rahmen des „Global Doll Kongresses" vom 30. September bis 2. Oktober 1983 in Limburg. Teilnehmer aus England, USA, Deutschland, der Schweiz, Frankreich, Niederlande, Spanien, Belgien, Österreich, Australien, Irland, Südafrika, Kanada und Schweden hatten sich angemeldet. Am ersten Tag fand eine Sightseeing-Tour mit Dampferfahrt auf dem Rhein statt, am zweiten konnte man verschiedene Workshops besuchen, u.a. referierte Guiseppe Garella aus Italien über die Geschichte der Lenci-Puppen, François Theimer über französische Puppen, Ingrid Scheinhard über antike Puppenhäuser und Puppenstuben-Puppen. Carol Ann Stan-

bitors from seven countries were present. And there was a special section for artistic dolls and reproductions. Admittedly participation in the competition was open to all G.D.S. members, but in order to ensure a fairer assessment, both the main groups were divided up into two sub-groups, and to be more precise, into professional and amateur doll-makers. Artistic dolls were submitted in main group 1, and were awarded, in the event of winning, a blue sash. Miniature dolls up to 20 cm, were in category 1, and porcelain dolls were entered in category 2. At that time the head for porcelain dolls had to be made of porcelain, the limbs could be made of other materials. The rules were not as strict then as they are today. Dolls of different materials, except porcelain, were put together into category 3. All in all 185 dolls were entered. „It was a pleasure to discover so many outstanding submissions

33

Morgiane, Unikat,
1989.
*Morgiane,
Onl-of-a-Kind, 1989.*

34

Unikat, 1989. Die Puppe hat eine Stockpuppe der Künstlerin Sylvia Wanke in der Hand. *One-of-a-kind 1989. In her hand the doll is holding a stick doll made by the artist Sylvia Wanke.*

35

G.D.S. - Kongreß in Heidelberg, 1988. Vorführung zum Thema „Modellieren eines Puppenkopfes", hier begutachtet von Renate Höckh.

G.D.S. convention in Heidelberg 1988. Demonstration on the topic "Modelling a doll's head" studied here by Renate Höckh.

ton berichtete über sammelnswerte Teddybären, (die nach wie vor ihre Leidenschaft sind, wie Sie noch erfahren werden), Jackie Jacobs über antike Puppenkleider und Zubehör, Simone Monville und Margaret Glover referierten über Restaurationsmöglichkeiten antiker Puppen und Laura Shreeve demonstrierte, wie man Perücken knüpft. Astry Campbell hielt einen Vortrag über amerikanische Künstlerpuppen.

Am dritten Tag der Convention, dem 2. Oktober 1983, fand außer dem „I. Puppenwettbewerb in Europa" auch die mittlerweile VIII. Frankfurter Puppenbörse im Hotel „Frankfurter Hof" statt. Über 80 Aussteller aus sieben Ländern waren vertreten. Und es gab eine Spezialabteilung für Künstlerpuppen und Reproduktionen.

Zwar stand die Teilnahme am Wettbewerb allen G.D.S.-Mitgliedern frei, doch, um eine gerechtere Beurteilung zu gewährleisten, wurden die beiden Hauptgruppen in zwei Untergruppen eingeteilt, und zwar in berufsmäßige Puppenmacher und Amateure. Künstlerpup-

amongst the artistic dolls" wrote the „Puppen Brief" in November 1983. All G.D.S. members were entitled to vote. On average 200 votes were cast for each category and group. The dolls with the most votes won. Hildegard Günzel had been preparing herself for this opportunity for weeks, and, „made an all-out effort, summoning up all my experience and skill". She was excited when she entered the hall of the „Frankfurt Hof", doll in hand, which she carried both with pride and caution. The first person she met was Annette Himstedt. Both suffered an equal shock, for this was the competition, and they knew each other. Both were afraid, because each knew the high quality of the other's dolls. „We didn't know then, that we would bump into each other again and again, and to be more precise, all over the world". Rotraut Schrott also took part in this first G.D.S. competition. Both Hildegard Günzel and Rotraut Schrott won first prize that day, Rotraut Schrott in category 3 „Non-porcelain/professional" and Hildegard Günzel in category 2 „ Porcelain

Unikat, 1988.
One-of-a-kind, 1988.

Puppe zum Thema Comedia de l`Arte.

Comedia de l'Arte dolls.

1. Signierstunde.
1st signing.

pen wurden in der Hauptgruppe I eingereicht und erhielten - falls sie siegten - eine blaue Schärpe. In der Kategorie 1 waren Miniaturpuppen bis 20 cm, in Kategorie 2 Porzellanpuppen vertreten. Bei den Porzellanpuppen mußte damals der Kopf aus Porzellan sein, die Gliedmaßen konnten aus anderen Materialien bestehen. Damals waren die Regeln noch nicht so streng wie heute. In Kategorie 3 waren Puppen aus unterschiedlichen Materialien, außer Porzellan, zusammengefaßt. Insgesamt waren 185 Puppen eingereicht worden. „Es war ein Vergnügen, so viele hervorragende Einlieferungen unter den Künstlerpuppen zu entdecken", schrieb der „Puppen-Brief" im November 1983. Wahlberechtigt waren alle G.D.S. Mitglieder. Durchschnittlich entfielen auf jede Kategorie und Gruppe etwa 200 Stimmen. Die Puppen mit den jeweils meisten Stimmen gewannen.

dolls/professional". Annette Himstedt was second. First of all Hildegard Günzel couldn't believe it. But then Annette Himstedt came over and said „Hildegard, you have won".
„That was the first competition and the first prize in my life". Many were still to follow.
Of course this event was covered by the media. Again it was the „Brigitte" magazine, which had already taken an active part in doll events, which came up to Hildegard Günzel and asked, whether she would also make portrait dolls. Obviously it was for a report, covering the creation of a doll modelled on a living model. „Then" said Hildegard Günzel later „Emma", elitist that I was, I made a possibly decisive error. I responded to the question, „Well, but that's boring". Why don't you do fairy tale dolls ! „Brigitte" then asked Annette Himstedt, who promptly agreed.
Today Hildegard Günzel knows that her decision at that time was instinctively the right one. „For I was travelling in another direction, not too close to people, I didn't want that ! Making portraits, that means making imitations, which didn't seem professional enough to me at the time". The prize doll of the first G.D.S. competition had to survive some moves in the subsequent period. In Kuppenheim, Hildegard Günzel's last „House of Dolls" in which she worked until 1994, the doll was dismantled. Her hair and her clothes were washed. They have turned out to be very beautiful once more, and are unfortunately, all that is left of the doll. In the confusion of the move the parts were lost. Only pictures still exist of the first great success in Hildegard Günzel's career as a doll artist. What a shame ! In the period following this, Hildegard Günzel went on working together with Wanke, and had a stand at all his exchanges. 1984 brought her not only more successes and prizes, it was also the year in which she finally said farewell to using cernite as a material, which she was still using for modelling up to that time. This is thanks to the American doll-artist Astry Campbell who finally dissuaded

Hildegard Günzel hatte sich auf diese Gelegenheit wochenlang vorbereitet und „alles, was ich konnte, aus mir herausgeholt". Sie war aufgeregt, als sie den Saal des „Frankfurter Hofs" betrat, ihre Puppe im Arm, die sie stolz und behutsam trug. Die erste, die sie traf, war Annette Himstedt. Beide bekamen gleichermaßen einen Schreck, denn dies war Konkurrenz, die man kannte. Und fürchtete, denn jede kannte die Qualität der Puppen der anderen. „Damals wußten wir noch nicht, daß wir uns immer wieder über den Weg laufen würden, und zwar an jedem Ort der Welt". Auch Rotraut Schrott nahm an diesem ersten G.D.S. Wettbewerb teil. Beide, Hildegard Günzel und Rotraut Schrott haben an diesem Tag 1. Preise gewonnen, Rotraut Schrott in Kategorie 3: „Nicht-Porzellan/Professionals" und Hildegard Günzel in der Kategorie 2 „Porzellanpuppen/Professionals" . Annette Himstedt wurde Zweite. Zuerst wollte Hildegard Günzel es nicht glauben. „Doch dann kam Annette Himstedt und sagte: „Hildegard, du hast gewonnen!" Das war der 1. Wettbewerb und der 1. Preis in meinem Leben". Noch viele sollten folgen.

Natürlich war auch die Presse an diesem Tag vertreten. Wieder war es das Magazin „Brigitte", das an dem Puppengeschehen bereits früher regen Anteil genommen hatte, das auf Hildegard Günzel zukam und fragte, ob sie auch Porträtpuppen machen würde. Offensichtlich ging es um eine Reportage, in deren Verlauf eine Puppe nach einem lebendigen Vorbild geschaffen werden sollte. „Damals", sagte Hildegard Günzel später, „machte ich, „Emma"-elitär, wie ich war, einen möglicherweise entscheidenden Fehler: Ich antwortete auf die Frage: „Also, das ist doch langweilig. Machen Sie doch lieber Märchenpuppen!" „Brigitte" fragte dann Annette Himstedt, und

Unikat, 1987. Der erste Versuch, die Puppen mit mehr fotographischer Rafinesse darzustellen.
One-of a-kind 1987. The first attempt to make the dolls more photogenic.

her from using it. She was holding a seminar in Limburg to which ten German doll-artists had travelled to take part. Hildegard Günzel was one of them. Also present were Rotraut Schrott and Karin Lossnitzer, who are both well known for their enchanting dolls made of cernite. At that time the 'Puppenbrief' 2/III Quarter of 1984 wrote „Astry Campbell introduced the seminar participants to the art of porcelain doll manufacture with a great deal of subject knowledge and commitment. The task set for the participants was to model a head either to a copy or to their own design. Perhaps it should be said at this point that these are certainly the only such courses to be held in Europe. Astry Campbell is a skilled artist who is happy to pass on her wealth of experience" but „Precise craftsmanship and concentration are required". Astry Campbell, a perfectionist, did not tolerate any inaccuracies". The special thing here was the fact that Astry Campbell was using plasticine for modelling, a material which was until then unknown to Hildegard Günzel. „Up to that point in time I had stubbornly stuck to my old ways". She enjoyed using plasticine. Astry Campbell observed this and allowed her to go ahead. She hadn't talked her into working with it. From now on all Günzel dolls were modelled with plasticine. After 1984 Hildegard Günzel's changed direction again. The reason for this new development was the second G.D.S. convention in Luzern in Switzerland, held from the 5th to the 7th of October 1984. Once again she won the gold prize. „Marion" was the name of the prize doll which was the delight of the collectors. Moreover she was the first version of „Cinderella" to be coated with wax, and more will be written about her at a later time. Everyone wanted to have her but Hildegard Günzel didn't want to sell her. Then in conversation with Matthias Wanke came the decisive brain wave, the spark which virtually set light to an area conflagration of doll making „Why don't we make a cast of it and use it for

diese sagte prompt zu. Heute weiß Hildegard Günzel, daß ihre Entscheidung damals instinktiv richtig war, „ denn ich ging ja einen anderen Weg, nicht zu nahe am Menschen, das wollte ich nicht! Porträts machen, also etwas nachahmen, erschien mir damals nicht professionell genug".

Die Preispuppe des 1. G.D.S.-Wettbewerbs mußte in der Folgezeit einige Umzüge überstehen. In Kuppenheim, Hildegard Günzels letztem Puppenhaus, in dem sie bis 1994 arbeitete, wurde sie auseinandergenommen. Ihre Haare wurden gewaschen und ihre Kleider. Sie sind wieder sehr schön geworden und leider alles, was von der Puppe noch übrig ist. In den Wirren des Umzuges gingen die Teile verloren. Nur Bilder existieren noch von dem ersten großen Erfolg in Hildegard Günzels Puppenkünstler-Karriere. Schade!

In der Folgezeit arbeitete Hildegard Günzel weiter mit Wanke zusammen und war auf allen seinen Börsen vertreten. Das Jahr 1984 brachte ihr nicht nur weitere Erfolge und Preise, es war auch das Jahr, in dem sie sich endgültig von dem Material Cernit verabschiedete, das sie bis dahin noch immer beim Modellieren verwendete. Es ist der amerikanischen Puppenkünstlerin Astry Campbell zu verdanken, die sie schließlich davon abbrachte. Sie leitete ein Seminar in Limburg, zu dem zehn deutsche Puppenkünstlerinnen angereist kamen. Hildegard Günzel war unter ihnen. Anwesend waren auch Rotraut Schrott und Karin Lossnitzer, die beide für ihre zauberhaften Puppen aus Cernit bekannt sind. Der „Puppen-Brief" 2/III. Quartal 1984 schrieb damals: „... Astry Campbell führte die Teilnehmer mit viel Sachkenntnis und Engagement in die hohe Schule der Porzellanpuppenherstellung ein. Die Aufgabe der Teilnehmer bestand darin, einen Kopf entweder nach Vorlage oder nach eigener Phantasie zu modellieren. ... Vielleicht sollte an dieser Stelle gesagt werden, daß es sicher in Europa einmalig ist, daß solche Kurse abgehalten werden. Astry Campbell ist eine versierte Künstlerin, die ihren großen

Baby Helga, erfolgreiche Puppenform.
Baby Helga, a successful commercial mold.

holding seminars"? After the initial euphoria Hildegard Günzel became reflective. What will happen if we sell the cast? If anyone with an inclination to do so can copy a Günzel doll? What will they look like? Will they still be Günzel doll-children? And what, if other lady doll makers with little experience of modelling make small amendments to the cast and themselves produce 'real' Günzel dolls or dolls à la Hildegard Günzel? That could possibly result in serious financial consequences for Hildegard Günzel. This was therefore a decision which required some thinking about and the most careful checking. Hildegard Günzel voiced her misgivings. But Matthias Wanke was enthusiastic about it and did not want to give in now. After some toing and froing she gave in, and reluctantly gave him two models, one puppet and one clown. Matthias Wanke found these very nice it is true, but he nevertheless insisted on „Marion". Stubbornly he continued to negotiate and refused to let himself be brushed off. With a sigh, Hildegard Günzel finally gave way, so three Günzel models went into production straight away at

Erfahrungsschatz gerne weitergibt...", aber: „...Genaues handwerkliches Arbeiten und Konzentration sind notwendig... Astry Campbell, eine Perfektionistin, ließ keine Ungenauigkeit zu...". Das Besondere dabei war, daß Astry Campbell zum Modellieren Plastilin verwendete, ein Material, das Hildegard Günzel bis dahin nicht kannte. „Ich hatte bis zu diesem Zeitpunkt bocksköpfig am Alten festgehalten". Die Sache machte ihr Spaß. Astry Campbell sah es und ließ sie machen; sie hat ihr nicht in die Arbeit hineingeredet. Von nun an wurden alle Günzel-Puppen aus Plastilin modelliert.

Nach 1984 änderte sich der Weg der Künstlerin erneut. Auslöser für die neue Entwicklung war die 2. G.D.S. Convention in Luzern/Schweiz vom 5. Bis 7. Oktober 1984. Wieder gewann sie Gold.

„Marion" hieß die Preispuppe, die das Entzücken der Sammler war. Übrigens war sie die mit Wachs überzogene erste Version der „Cinderella", über die an anderer Stelle berichtet wird. Jeder wollte sie haben, aber die Puppenkünstlerin wollte sie nicht verkaufen. Dann - im Gespräch mit Matthias Wanke - der entscheidende Geistesblitz, der Funke, der geradezu einen Flächenbrand des Puppenmachens auslöste: „Warum machen wir denn nicht davon eine Form? Und halten damit Seminare ab?!"

Nach der ersten Euphorie kamen Hildegard Günzel doch Bedenken. Was wird passieren, wenn wir die Form verkaufen? Wenn jeder, der möchte, eine Günzel-Puppe nacharbeiten kann? Wie werden sie aussehen? Werden das immer noch Günzel-Puppenkinder sein? Und was, wenn andere, Puppenmacherinnen mit wenig Erfahrung im Modellieren, die Form geringfügig verändern und nun ihrerseits „echte" Günzel-Puppen oder Puppen à la Hildegard Günzel produzieren? Unter Umständen könnten sich daraus gravierende finanzielle Nachteile für sie ergeben. Dies war also eine Entscheidung, die einiges Nachdenken und sorgfältigste Prüfung erforderte. Hildegard

the Wanke company. „Marion" was the first artistic doll of which a cast was made and sold. Mind you, with the new name of „Georgia". A German doll company had objected to the use of the name „Marion". At the beginning of 1985 the first casts were available which admittedly still had the old name „Marion", so that many buyers thought that they had received the wrong cast. In the following period the Wanke company achieved a large proportion of its turnover with this doll model (the sleeping baby „Jenny „ was also very popular, not only because it was easy to finish

Im Kreis ihrer Puppen, 1986. Noch sind alle Puppen Unikate.
Surrounded by her dolls, 1986. These are still all one-of-a-kind dolls.

Günzel äußerte ihre Befürchtungen. Doch Matthias Wanke hatte Feuer gefangen und wollte nun nicht mehr nachgeben. Nach einigem Hin und Her ließ sie sich breitschlagen und gab ihm - widerstrebend - zwei Modelle: eine Marionette und einen Bajazzo. Das fand Matthias Wanke zwar sehr nett, doch er bestand trotzdem auf „Marion" . Hartnäckig verhandelte er weiter und ließ sich nicht abwimmeln. Seufzend gab sie schließlich nach. So gingen gleich drei Günzel-Modelle bei der Firma Wanke in Produktion. „Marion" war die erste Künstlerpuppe, die abgeformt und verkauft wurde - allerdings unter der neuen Bezeichnung „Georgina". Eine deutsche Puppenfirma hatte gegen die Verwendung des Namens „Marion" Einspruch erhoben. Anfang 1985 lagen die ersten Formen vor, in denen allerdings noch die alte Bezeichnung „Marion" stand, so daß viele Käufer glaubten, die falsche Form erhalten zu haben. In der Folgezeit wurde mit diesem Puppenmodell ein Großteil des Umsatzes der Firma Wanke erzielt. (Sehr beliebt, nicht nur, weil es von Anfängern leicht nachgearbeitet werden konnte, war später auch das schlafende Baby „Jenny".) 1985 schloß Hildegard Günzel einen Vertrag mit Matthias Wanke.

Von nun an sollte es Wochen und Monate geben, in denen sie fast mehr Zeit im Flugzeug als an ihrem Arbeitsplatz oder zu Hause verbringen würde. Heute entsteht manch eine Günzel-Puppe „im Fluge". Nicht nur, daß die vielen Köpfe, die sie gestaltet hat, sie bei der Arbeit sehr schnell gemacht haben: Hildegard Günzel bleibt tatsächlich manchmal nichts anderes übrig, als mit einem Block Plastilin im Handgepäck zu reisen und lange Interkontinentalflüge zu nutzen, um Köpfe zu modellieren.

for beginners). In 1985 Hildegard Günzel signed a contract with Matthias Wanke. From now on Hildegard Günzel's life and career ran at an even quicker tempo. This was due, amongst other things, to always being a passenger in Matthias Wanke's car on trips to European destinations. He drove at breakneck speed and loved to cross Germany in two hours like an Intercity train. Hildegard Günzel hates very fast driving and on occasions thought she was going to die. The more she complained, the more Matthias laughed. But these trips were nothing compared to the journeys now demanded of her. From now on there would be weeks and months in which she virtually spent more time on board an aeroplane than at work or at home. Today many a Günzel doll is an in-flight creation. Not only have the many heads which she has shaped made her very quick at this work, Hildegard Günzel sometimes actually has no choice but to travel with a strip of plasticine in her hand luggage and use the long inter-continental flights to model heads. Günzel dolls are part of the Jet Set.

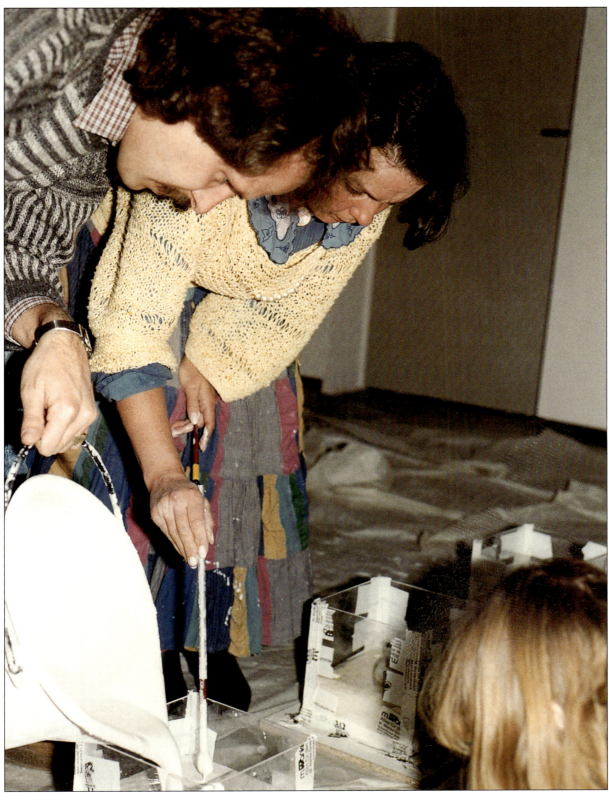

Erstes Seminar bei der Firma Wanke in Limburg,
1985.

First seminar held at the Wanke company in Limburg,
1985.

Günzel-Puppen werden international
Günzel dolls turning internationel

„Georgina" wurde weltweit vertrieben. Bald war der Name „Hildegard Günzel" auch auf anderen Kontinenten Sammlern ein Begriff. Die Puppenkünstlerin reiste mit Matthias Wanke um die Welt und hielt Vorträge, zeigte selbstproduzierte Videos und begeisterte viele Menschen für Künstlerpuppen. Stationen in diesem Jahr waren die Schweiz, die Niederlande, England, Australien, Neuseeland und die USA.

In England, genauer gesagt in Brighton, fand am 19. Oktober 1985 der 3. Jahreswettbewerb der G.D.S. statt. In der ersten Ausgabe, Nr. 1/86 des „Mitglieder-Magazins" der G.D.S., das von da an viermal jährlich erscheinen sollte, berichtete Carol Stanton, daß 250 Teilnehmer aus 17 Ländern anwesend waren. Immer mehr Menschen interessierten sich für Puppen. Der „Puppen-Brief", für den Matthias Wanke inzwischen allein verantwortlich zeichnete, war mittlerweile farbig geworden und hatte nun eine Auflage von 50.000! Immer noch galt das Hauptinteresse der Mitglieder den antiken Puppen, wie eine damals erfolgte Umfrage bewies. An zweiter Stelle folgten Künstlerpuppen. Für Reproduktionen von antiken Puppen, mit denen ja alles angefangen hatte, interessierten sich zu diesem Zeitpunkt schon deutlich weniger Personen. Wie immer, begann die Convention mit einer Besichtigungstour. Man fuhr nach Windsor Castle und betrachtete das prächtige Puppenhaus der Queen Mary. Als Mittagessen gab es ein typisch englisches Menü in der Lodge vom Windsor Safari Park. Der Kongress selbst wurde im Seebad Brighton, im direkt am Meer gelegenen Hotel Metropole, abgehalten. Lichtbildervorträge wurden am Samstag gezeigt, u.a. von Dorothy Coleman, der „großen alten Dame" der Puppenszene aus den USA, deren „Collector's Encyclopedia of Dolls" die An-

„Georgia" was sold throughout the world. Soon the name „Hildegard Günzel" was a byword for collectors in other continents. Hildegard Günzel travelled around the world with Matthias Wanke and gave lectures, showed videos taken by herself and aroused the interest of many people in artistic dolls. This year visits were made to Switzerland, the Netherlands, England, Australia, New Zealand and the USA. The 3rd annual G.D.S. competition was held on 19th October 1985. In England, Brighton to be

Helfer im Puppenhaus, 1993.
Assistant in the House of Dolls, 1993.

Hildegard Günzel und Uschi Creyels.
Hildegard Günzel and Uschi Creyels.

tiksammler einen Großteil ihres Wissens über ihr Sammelgebiet verdanken. Hildegard Günzel zeigte einen Video-Film über ihre Arbeit.

280 Puppen waren für den Wettbewerb eingereicht worden, die es zu dekorieren galt. Mit viel Liebe und Sorgfalt kümmerten sich Debbie Stanton und ihre Helfer um die Wettbewerbs-Schönheiten. Unter der Rubrik „Künstlerpuppen" gab es inzwischen 7 Kategorien; eine zusätzliche waren „Stofftiere", die man damals offensichtlich weder zu trennen, noch einzuordnen wußte. Alle 8 Kategorien waren wie immer in die Untergruppen „Professionals" und „Amateure" geteilt. Die Gewinnerliste dieses Wettbewerbs liest sich heute wie ein „Who´s who der Puppenkunst": In der Kategorie 1 - Porzellan: 1. . M. Armstrong-Hand, USA; 2. Renate Höckh, Deutschland; 3. Carol Stanton, England. Karin Schmidt wurde damals noch als „Amateur" geführt und bekam den 3. Preis. Hildegard Günzel gewann auch hier einen 1. Preis, und zwar in der Kategorie 2 - Wachs. Gillie Charlson aus England errang den zweiten und Renate Höckh den dritten Preis der Professionals in dieser Kategorie. Weitere Teilnehmer, die Preise gewannen, waren Wiltrud Stein, Barbara Aalrust, Irmgard Becker, Ingrid Winter, Patty Hale und andere. Namen, die heute in der Szene jeder kennt.

Kurz vor Beginn des festlichen Abendessens traf eine Gruppe aufgeregter und offensichtlich verärgerter, alle in reizende Kimonos gekleideter, japanischer Puppenmacherinnen ein, die von den Anwesenden mit herzlichem Applaus begrüßt wurden. Ein durcheinander geratener Reiseplan hatte ihnen die Teilnahme am Wettbewerb vermasselt! Kurz entschlossen wurde für die Delegation aus dem Land der aufgehenden Sonne ein Extra-Wettbewerb angesetzt, damit sie die lange Reise um die halbe Welt mit ihren Puppen nicht umsonst gemacht hatten. Er fand am Tag danach statt, und alle Mitglieder beteiligten sich noch ein-

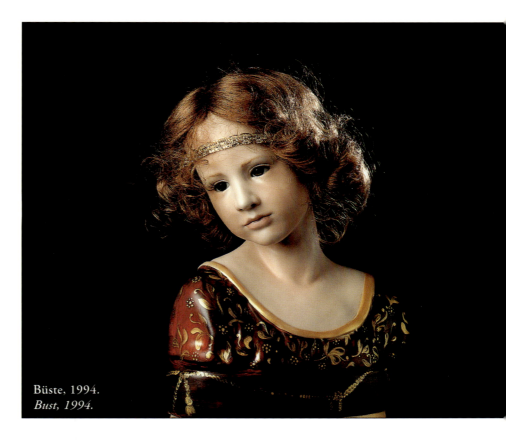

Büste, 1994.
Bust, 1994.

Büste mit Taube, 1991.
Bust with dove, 1991.

mal am Wahlgeschehen. Selbstverständlich wurden die Gewinner auch mit Medaillen ausgezeichnet. Abschließend wurden die Puppen noch einmal der Öffentlichkeit präsentiert. Eine schöne Geste der Veranstalter, die ihrem Motto „Weltweite Freundschaft durch Puppen" gerecht wurde.

Nun wurden Günzel-Puppen erstmalig auch in Australien ausgestellt. Sie erzielten den 1. Preis der „Gold Coast Company" in Brisbane und den 1. Preis (Gold) des 1. G.D.S. Kongresses in Australien, der vom 20. Bis 23. Juni 1986 in Sydney stattfand. Tagungsort war das „Hilton"-Hotel. Die Kongreßbesucher kamen aus allen Teilen des Kontinents, einige sogar aus Neuseeland, angereist. Am ersten Tag wurden Workshops abgehalten, am folgenden Tag Lichtbildervorträge vorgeführt. Jackie Jacobs,

more exact. In the first issue no. 1/86 of the G.D.S. „Member-magazine", which from then onwards was to appear four times a year, Carol Stanton reported that 250 participants from 17 countries attended. More and more people were developing an interest in dolls. The „Puppen-Brief" for which Matthias Wanke had in the meantime become solely responsible, had been printed in colour in the interim period and now had a circulation of 50,000 ! The main interest of the members remained antique dolls, as a survey conducted at that time established. In second place followed artistic dolls. Even at this point in time

Unikat, 1993, H. Günzel Unikat Show Toy-Building, 5th Avenue, New York.
One-of-a-kind, 1993, H.G.´s own
One-of-a-kind show, Toy Building. 5th Avenue, New York.

48

Unikat, 1993, ausgestellt
auf der eigenen Unikat-
Austellung.
*One-of-a-kind, 1993,
Hildegard Günzel's own
one-of-a-kind show, Toy
Building, 5th Avenue,
New York.*

Carol Ann Stanton und Nick Allington aus England und Hildegard Günzel referierten über ihre Arbeit. Romy Roeder, Jackie Brooks, Wendy Richardson und Mart Fainges vertraten das Gastgeberland. Bei der Puppenbörse am Sonntag wurden mehr als tausend Besucher gezählt, und so zahlte sich die harte Arbeit aus, die Red und Janette Radcliffe für das Gelingen der Veranstaltung geleistet hatten.

Hildegard Günzel errang in Australien außerdem den Sonderpreis und einen Pokal für die „beste Idee".

Reisen in diesen Teil des Globus sind der Puppendesignerin besonders gut in Erinnerung geblieben, denn dabei sind einige Dinge passiert, die einfach im Gedächtnis haften bleiben. Einmal mußte sie allein reisen. Sonst war sie ja meistens mit Matthias Wanke und seiner „Puppenfamilie" zusammen. Damals, Mitte der achtziger Jahre, waren Fernreisen für sie jedoch noch nicht so selbstverständlich wie heute. Alleingelassen, fühlte sie sich sehr unsicher und schloß sich aus diesem Grund auf dem Frankfurter Flughafen an ein älteres Ehepaar an, das ebenfalls in diesen Teil der Welt unterwegs war. Das Ehepaar war sehr nett und verständnisvoll und kümmerte sich während des ganzen Fluges rührend um die damals noch nicht sehr „reisefeste" Puppenkünstlerin. Der Flug ging über Singapore, wo Hildegard Günzel die anderen treffen sollte. Bei der Ankunft war sie jedoch schon mutiger und verabredete tatendurstig mit dem Taxifahrer, der sie ins Hotel brachte, eine Stadtrundfahrt, die fünfzig Dollar kosten sollte. „Ich machte damals wirklich jeden Fehler, den man machen kann". Im Hotel angekommen, erfuhr sie an der Rezeption, daß so etwas normalerweise wesentlich weniger kostete, nämlich 15 Dollar. Vergeblich versuchte Hildegard Günzel dem Taxifahrer, der auf der Einhaltung der mündlichen Vereinbarung bestand, aus dem Weg zu gehen: Er stöberte sie überall auf. Schließlich gab sie entnervt auf und ihm als

markedly less people were interested in reproductions of antique dolls, with which it had indeed all started. As ever, the convention began with a sightseeing tour. There was a trip to Windsor Castle to look at the magnificent Queen Mary doll's house. For lunch there was typical English fare in the Windsor Safari Park Lodge. The congress itself was held in the seaside resort of Brighton, in the Metropole Hotel which is on the sea front. Slide lectures were shown on the Saturday, amongst others by Dorothy Coleman, the grand old lady of the doll scene in the USA, and to whose „Collector's Encyclopaedia of Dolls" antique collectors owe a large amount of their knowledge about their hobby. Hildegard Günzel showed a video film about her work. 280 dolls had been submitted for the competition, which was to be judged and prizes awarded for the winners. Debbie Stanton and her assistants looked after the competition beauties with a great deal of love and care. In the meantime there was a total of 7 categories under the heading „artistic dolls"; plus an additional one for „Soft toys" - at that time it was evidently not known how to divide or group them. As always, all 8 categories were divided up into the sub-groups. „Professionals" and „Amateurs". Today the list of winners of this competition reads like a „Who's Who" of artistic dolls. In category 1 - porcelain. First M. Armstrong - Hand USA, second Renate Häckh, Germany; third, Carol Stanton, England. Karin Schmidt was at that time still entered under „Amateurs" and was awarded third prize. Here too Hildegard Günzel won a first prize, and to be more precise in category 2 - wax. Gillie Charlson from England carried off second, and Renate Häckh third prize for professionals in this sector. Other participants who won prizes were

Unikat, 1993, im Toy-Building, 5th Avenue, New York.
ONe-of-a-kind, 1993, Toy Building, 5th Avenue, New York.

50

Unikat 1993, Nürnberg.
*One-of-a-kind, 1993,
Nuremberg.*

Puppenhaus in Duisburg, 1994, 1000 qm für Produktion und Museum. Das Gebäude wurde mit zwei Architekturpreisen für den Architekten Christian Kohl ausgezeichnet.

House of Dolls in Duisburg, 1994. 1000 m2 provides accommodation for production and a museum. The architect Christian Kohl was awarded two architectural prizes for the building.

Entschädigung 10 Dollar, worauf sie ihn endlich los wurde.

Eine weitere Begebenheit, an die sie sich lachend erinnert, geschah ebenfalls während eines Kongresses in Australien. Die Besucher standen nach ihrem Vortrag mit den Programmheften in der Hand vor Hildegard Günzel Schlange. Die Künstlerin strahlte sie an, konnte sich jedoch nicht erklären, was sie von ihr wollten, bis Matthias Wanke, der grinsend zugeschaut hatte, sagte: „Sie möchten, daß Sie sie signieren". Das hat sie dann auch mit Begeisterung getan. Sie freute sich so sehr darüber, daß es Menschen gab, die teilweise weite Strecken zurückgelegt hatten, um ein Autogramm von ihr zu erhalten, daß sie damit nicht eher aufhören wollte, bis alle zufrieden gestellt waren. Erst, als Matthias Wanke ungeduldig wurde und sagte: „ Also, ich denke, Sie sollten jetzt langsam Schluß machen, die an-

Wiltrud Stein, Barbara Aalrust, Irmgard Becker, Ingrid Winter, Patty Hale, and others. Names known to everyone in the scene today. Shortly before the beginning of the festive evening meal, a group of excited and evidently angry Japanese lady doll-makers all dressed in pretty kimonos arrived, who were greeted with warm applause from those present. A muddle in the itinerary had prevented them from taking part in the competition. Without a moment's hesitation it was decided to hold an extra competition for the delegation from the land of the rising sun, so that they would not have made the long journey half way round the world with their dolls in vain. It took place on the following day, and all members took part in the voting again. Of course the winners were also awarded medals. At the end the dolls were shown off to the public again. A nice gesture by the organisers, who

deren Redner wollen auch noch etwas sagen", merkte sie, daß sie drauf und dran war, den Veranstaltungs-Zeitplan durcheinander zu bringen. Trotzdem gab sie nicht gleich auf und sagte: „Ach, lassen Sie mich doch noch ein bißchen machen, wer weiß, ob ich je im Leben noch einmal dazu komme!"

Im Anschluß sollte es von Australien nach Neuseeland gehen, um Vorbereitungen für den Kongreß im nächsten Jahr zu besprechen. Matthias Wanke hatte dazu keine rechte Lust. Er war sehr müde, denn die Reise war anstrengend verlaufen. Hildegard Günzel sagte zum ihm: „Seien Sie doch froh, daß Sie so tolle Reisen machen können". Darauf antwortete er: „Fliegen Sie doch mit". Sie wußte nicht so recht, ob sie sich das leisten konnte, denn schließlich mußte sie alle Reisen selbst finanzieren, und damals stand sie erst am Anfang ihrer Puppenmacher-Karriere. Aber Matthias Wanke sagte: „Von Australien aus ist das nicht weit. Neuseeland ist eine vorgelagerte Insel. Nur ein Katzensprung". Der Katzensprung dauerte mehrere Stunden und kostete weit über 1.000.– Mark. Die Puppenkünstlerin bekam einen Schreck, denn damit hatte sie nicht gerechnet. Und nicht mit so hohen Kosten.

Als sie im kommenden Jahr in Nelson ankamen, wurden sie von den dortigen G.D.S. Mitgliedern herzlich empfangen. Neuseeland mit seiner klaren Luft und der reizvollen Landschaft machte damals einen großen Eindruck auf die drei Reisenden aus dem fernen Europa. 166 Teilnehmer waren auf dem Kongreß vertreten, und mehr als doppelt so viele besuchten die Puppenbörse am Sonntag. Wenn man die geringe Einwohnerzahl Neuseelands und die weiten Entfernungen bedenkt, ist das eine beachtliche Zahl.

Auch hier wurde eine Puppe von Hildegard Günzel mit „Gold" ausgezeichnet.

Das neue Gebäude bietet modernste Produktionstechnik.
The new building houses the most up-to-date production-technology.

justified their motto „Global friendship through dolls". Now Günzel dolls were exhibited in Australia for the first time. They won first prize from the „Gold Coast Company" in Brisbane and first prize (Gold) at the G.D.S. congress in Australia, which was held from the 20th to the 23rd of June 1986 in Sydney. The „Hilton" hotel was the venue. The congress visitors came from all over the continent, some even travelled from New Zealand. Workshops were held on the first day, and on the following day slide lectures were given. Jackie Jacobs, Carol Ann Stanton, and Nick Allington from England, and Hildegard Günzel lectured on their work. Romy Roeder, Jackie Brooks, Wendy Richardson and Mart Fainges represented the host country. More than a thousand visitors were counted at the doll exchange on Sunday, thus the hard work by Red and Janette Radcliffe had put into making the event a success paid off. In addition Hildegard Günzel won the special prize and a cup in Australia for the „best idea". Hildegard Günzel has particularly vivid memories of trips in this part of the globe, because certain events occurred here which simply stick in one's memory. Once she had to travel alone. Otherwise she mostly travelled together in fact with Matthias Wanke and his „doll family". At that time, in the mid eigh-

56 Schneewittchen und die sieben Zwerge, 1994, limitiert 4 Exemplare.

Snow White and the Seven Dwarfs, 1994, production limited to 4 samples.

Alice im Wunder-
land, 1994, limitiert
10 Exemplare.
*Alice in Wonderland,
1994, production
limited to 10 spieces.*

Mia, 1994, limitiert je 25 Exemplare
Europa/USA.
*Mia, 1994, production limited to 25 samples each for
Europe/USA.*

Lieschen, 1994, limitiert je 25 Exemplare
Europa/USA.
*Lieschen, 1994, production limited to 25 samples
each for Europe/USA.*

Marie Luise und Charlotte, 1994, limitiert
je 25 Exemplare Europa/USA (rechts).
*Marie Luise and Charlotte ,1994. production limited to
25 samples each for Europe/USA (right)*

Gretchen, Unikat,
1994.
*Gretchen,
One-of-a-kind, 1994.*

60

Unikat, 1994.
One-of-a-kind, 1994.

Unikat, 1994 (oben).
One-of-a-kind, 1994.

Unikat, 1994 (oben links).
One-of-a-kind, 1994.

Tina, 1994, limitiert je 25 Exemplare Europa/USA.
Tina, 1994, production limited to 25 samples each to Europe/USA.

Gruppe, 1994, je 25 Exemplare, Europa/USA,
4 Porzellanpuppen v.l.: (blaues Kleid) Anna, Beate,
Sandra, sitzend Rita (rechts).
Group, 1994, 25 samples of each group 4 porcelain dolls from left (blue dress) Anna, Beate, Sandra, Rita seated.

Promotiontour 1991 in den USA.

Signing tour in the USA, 1991.

Ein kleiner Teddybär sorgte während dieser Reise für zusätzliche Aufregung. Er hieß „Benjamin" und gehörte Carol Stanton, die ihn auf allen ihren Reisen ständig bei sich trug. Benjamin war nur 10 cm groß, dabei aber ausgesprochen unternehmungslustig. Mehr als einmal jammerte Carol Stanton über den - vermeintlichen - Verlust ihres Teddybären. Ganz fest nahm sie sich vor, auf ihn aufzupassen - vergebens! Sie packte ihn schließlich in ihren Kulturbeutel, den sie im Handgepäck im Flugzeug immer bei sich hatte. Die Heimreise ging damals wieder über Singapore. Alle drei, Hildegard Günzel, Carol Stanton und Matthias Wanke, schlenderten durch die Flughafenhalle und guckten mal in dieses, mal in jenes Geschäft. Dann, beim Einstiegen in die Maschine, erstarrte Carol. Der Beutel war weg! Und, was schlimmer war: Benjamin war weg! Sie machte auf dem Absatz kehrt. Mat-

ties, long haul journeys were not yet matter of course for her as they are today. Left on her own, she felt very insecure and therefore latched on to an older couple at Frankfurt airport who were likewise travelling to the same part of the world. The couple were very kind and understanding and looked after the „Doll artist", who was not as yet used to travelling, for the whole flight. The aeroplane touched down in Singapore, where Hildegard Günzel was supposed to meet the others. As she arrived in Singapore she had however drummed up her confidence and, hungry for action, she negotiated a trip around town with the taxi driver who took her to a hotel. This round trip was supposed to cost fifty dollars. „In those days I really made every mistake that it is possible to make". Arriving at the hotel, she learned at the reception that such a trip around town normally costed significantly less, name-

thias Wanke packte ihren Arm und rannte mit ihr den ganzen Weg zurück in die Abfertigungshalle. In einem Duty Free-Geschäft fanden sie dann tatsächlich beides wieder: Beutel und Bär. Hildegard Günzel stand indessen, unter den mißbilligenden Blicken der Stewardess, mit einem Fuß im Flugzeug, mit dem anderen draußen und war fest entschlossen, die Maschine so lange am Abflug zu hindern, bis alle wieder da waren. Carol Stanton entschloß sich daraufhin, den vorwitzigen Teddy in Zukunft zu Hause zu lassen.

Für den 4. Internationalen G.D.S.-Wettbewerb am 18.10. 1986 in der Mozartstadt Salzburg hatte sich die Künstlerin bereit erklärt, zusammen mit Astry Campbell die eingereichten Künstlerpuppen daraufhin zu überprüfen, daß keine im Handel erhältlichen Fertigteile wie Plastikmasken für Stoffpuppen oder aus gekauften Formen gegossene Puppengliedmaßen verwendet wurden. Die Wettbewerbsbedingungen waren inzwischen strenger als am Anfang. Jede Puppe mußte nun inklusive Kopf, Arme und Beine vom Künstler selbst entworfen sein.

Damals war es bei allen Puppenkünstlerinnen noch üblich, sogenannte „Vario"-Serien von Puppen zu fertigen. Es wurde nur eine Form gebaut und daraus unterschiedliche Puppen gefertigt. Man öffnete einer Puppe, die sonst geschlossene Lippen hatte, das Mündchen, machte den Augenausschnitt mal kleiner, mal größer und verwandte für unterschiedliche Puppen häufig die gleichen Hände und Füße, die aus diesem Grund stilisierter und weniger charakteristisch modelliert wurden. Jedoch wurden die Regeln immer strenger, die Standards immer höher. Dies ist gerade auch Hildegard Günzel zu verdanken, denn oftmals sind Neuerungen auf dem Künstlerpuppen-Gebiet mit dem Namen „Günzel" verknüpft. Viele haben davon profitiert, Puppenmacher wie Sammler. So modellierte sie 1985 als erste Puppenkünstlerin Puppen mit angewinkelten

ly 15 dollars. In vain Hildegard Günzel attempted to give the taxi driver, who insisted on that she keep her side of the verbal agreement, a wide berth. He followed her everywhere. Finally, she gave up and gave him 10 dollars in compensation, whereby she finally got rid of him. Another occurrence, which she remembers laughing, likewise took place at a congress in Australia. After her lecture the visi-

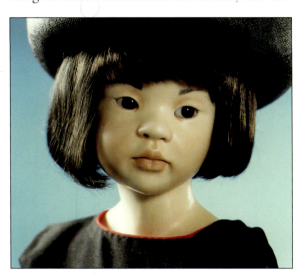

Keiko, 1995, limitiert je 35 Exemplare Europa/USA.
Keiko, 1995, production limited to 35 samples each for Europe/USA.

Yoko, 1995, limitiert je 35 Exemplare Europa/USA.
Yoko, 1995, production limited to 35 samples each for Europe/USA.

Valerie, 1995, limitiert
je 35 Exemplare Europa/
USA.
*Valerie, 1995, production
limited to 35 samples
each for Europe/USA.*

Daphne, 1995, limitiert je
35 Exemplare
Europa/USA.
*Daphne, 1995, production
limited to 35 samples each
for Europa/USA.*

Beinen und angeformten Knien. Ihre Puppen wurden dadurch noch „beweglicher". Sie hatten nun ein Spiel- und ein Standbein, eine Neuheit, die graziöse, tänzerische Stellungen genauso möglich machte wie das Sitzen. Hildegard Günzel hatte selbst zehn Jahre lang Ballettunterricht. Die damals erworbenen Kenntnisse beeinflußten nun ihre Arbeit. Bald darauf sah man auch von anderen Puppenmacherinnen Puppen in sitzender Stellung und mit angewinkelten Beinen. Hildegard Günzel findet es gut, daß sich viele in der Szene von ihr inspirieren ließen. Wenn eine neuartige Haltung - 1991 waren es aufgestützte Hände, die sie einführte - von anderen Puppenkünstlern für deren Puppen nachempfunden wurde, versteht sie das als Kompliment für ihre Arbeit. Sie ist anderen gegenüber offen und zugänglich, teilt ihre Erfahrungen bereitwillig mit ihnen und hat auch keine Angst, von anderen zu lernen. Konkurrenz ist wichtig. Wer seine Konkurrenz ernst nimmt, bringt ihr Re-

Zaide, 1995, limitiert 6 Exemplare.
Zaide, 1995, production limited to 6 samples.

Bonnie, 1995, limitiert je 25 Exemplare Europa/USA.
Bonnie, 1995, production limited to 25 samples each for Europe/USA.

tors, programme of events to hand, stood in a queue in front of Hildegard Günzel. Hildegard Günzel smiled at them, but could not however work out what they wanted from her, until Matthias Wanke, who had been looking on, grinning, said, „They would like you to give an autograph". Then she did so with enthusiasm, as well. She was so pleased that there were people, some of whom had travelled from afar for her autograph, that she didn't want to stop until she had given an autograph to all those who wanted one. Only when Matthias Wanke became impatient and said, „Well, I think you ought to start to wrap it up now, the other speakers also want to speak",

spekt entgegen. Eifersüchteleien sind nicht nach ihrem Geschmack. Sie sagt: „Ich bin harmoniesüchtig. Am liebsten möchte ich von allen Menschen geliebt werden!"

Hildegard Günzel ist ein Profi, doch Marketing mußte auch sie erst lernen. Damals, 1986, genoß sie es erst einmal, daß sie die Welt kennenlernen durfte. Sie staunte wie ein Kind und freute sich wie ein Schneekönig darüber, daß so viele Menschen unterschiedlichster Nationalitäten ihre Puppen liebten. Voraussetzung dafür war, „den gleichen Blick zu haben". Da gibt es offensichtlich keine Nationalitätsunterschiede: Ob Amerikaner, Japaner oder Deutsche - Liebhaber haben alle denselben Blick. Wenn die Puppenkünstlerin diesen Blick bei einer Frau sah, versuchte sie immer, ihr dabei zu helfen, die begehrte Puppe zu bekommen.

Unvergeßlich bleibt ihr die erste Reise nach New York.

did she notice that she was about to bring the event timetable into disarray. Inspite of this she didn't give up immediately and said, „Oh ! Let me just do a few more, who knows, whether I will ever get round to coming here again". Following this, the plan was to go from Australia to New Zealand to discuss the preparations for the congress in the following year. Matthias Wanke had no real inclination for this. He was very tired, because the trip had been trying. Hildegard Günzel said to him, „Just be happy that you can are in a position to undertake such great trips". Whereupon he replied „Fly there then". Hildegard Günzel wasn't really sure whether she could afford it, for she had to pay for all her flights herself and at that time she was only at the beginning of her career as a doll-maker. But Matthias Wanke said, „It's not far from Australia, New Zealand is an offshore island. Just a stone's throw from Australia". The sto-

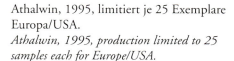

Athalwin, 1995, limitiert je 25 Exemplare Europa/USA.
Athalwin, 1995, production limited to 25 samples each for Europe/USA.

Einer der geheimnisvollen Ein- und Ausblicke im Puppenmuseum, im Hintergrund Lara, 1996 (rechts).
One of the secretive insights into and outlooks from the House of Dolls, with Lara in the background, 1996 (on the right).

Matthias Wanke hatte ihr vorgeschlagen, drei Puppen zur „Toy Fair" nach New York mitzunehmen, er sagte, er wüßte jemanden, der bereit wäre, die Puppen auf seinem Stand zu präsentieren.

„Als ich morgens beim Frühstück saß und sah, wie groß die Stadt ist, dachte ich: du bist wahnsinnig! Aber die Amerikaner sind total unkompliziert". Hildegard Günzel knüpfte schnell Kontakte zu Puppenmachern und Sammlern, die sie ihrerseits wieder in ihrem Bekanntenkreis „herumreichten". „Nach drei Stunden wußten alle auf der Ausstellung, wer Hildegard Günzel ist". 1986 erhielt sie den „Doty Award" des „Doll Reader" für „Cinderella". Und schon passierte ihr das Gleiche wie zwei Jahre zuvor mit „Marion". Wieder kam es zu einem Copyright-Konflikt. Die Firma Walt Disney machte freundlich, aber bestimmt klar, daß der Name „Cinderella" für sie geschützt und damit für alle anderen tabu sei. Die Puppe mußte umbenannt werden und hieß dann einfach „Milk Maid".

Doch New York wurde ein großer Erfolg. Mit dem „Doty Award" des Doll Reader und der Auszeichnung „Doll of Excellence" des Doll Magazine setzte der Günzel-Puppen-Boom in den USA ein. Matthias Wanke und Hildegard Günzel fuhren mit neuen Aufträgen in der Tasche nach Hause. Doch woher sollte sie das Geld nehmen, alle diese Aufträge auszuführen? Geschäfte in USA zu machen, ist eine ganz andere Sache als in Europa. Amerikanische Sammler legen Wert darauf, genau die Puppe zu erhalten, die sie geordert haben. „What you see is what you get!" Anders als in Deutschland, wo Sammler bestrebt sind, ein möglichst individuelles Stück zu erwerben und leichte Abweichungen in Farbe und Stoffqualität tolerieren, wäre so etwas in USA indiskutabel. Wenn eine Puppe auf 70 Exemplare limitiert ist, muß gewährleistet sein, daß auch für alle Puppen ausreichend Stoff von einer Qualität vorhanden ist. Klar, daß man sol-

Gretchen und Mephisto, 1994, Faust, Johann
Wolfgang v. Goethe.
*Gretchen and Mephisto, 1994, Faust, Johann
Wolfgang v. Goethe*

Elfe, 1996, limitiert 10 Exemplare.
Elf, 1996, production limited to 10 samples

Pauline, 1996, limitiert
je 35 Exemplare Europa/
USA.
*Pauline, 1996, produc-
tion limited to 35
samples each for Euro-
pe/USA.*

Anna May, 1996,
limitiert je 35 Exemplare
Europa/USA.
*Anna May 1996,
production limited to 35
samples each for Euro-
pe/USA.*

Fleurie, May Camée, Anemone, Rose, 1996, limitiert je 35 Exemplare Europa/USA.

Fleurie, May Camée, Anemone, Rose, 1996, production limited to 35 samples each for Europe/USA.

che Mengen nicht einfach im nächsten Laden kaufen kann. Heute kauft sie direkt bei den Herstellern ein und stellt dabei die Bedingung, daß sie die Qualität jederzeit nachordern kann. Damals,1986, war sie noch nicht soweit, deshalb wurde die in „Milk Maid" umbenannte „Cinderella" in verschiedene Stoffe gekleidet.

Nun zogen die Günzel-Puppen in ein größeres Studio. Das neue Puppenhaus war 200 qm groß und hatte zwei Stockwerke. In den vier Produktionsräumen des unteren Bereiches wurden Formen gelagert, es wurde gegossen, gesäubert und gebrannt. Die Fertigungs-, Büro- und Ausstellungsräume lagen im oberen Stock. In diesem Jahr waren Günzel-Puppen außer in Deutschland und USA auf Ausstellungen in Tokio, Australien und Neuseeland zu sehen.

ne's throw lasted several hours and costed much more than 1000 Deutsche Marks. Hildegard Günzel had a shock, for she had not reckoned that it would be so expensive and she didn't have much money on her. They were given a warm welcome in Nelson by the G.D.S. members there when they arrived in the following year. New Zealand with is clear air and attractive countryside made a big impression at that time on the three travellers from far away Europe. 166 participants attended the congress and more than double that number visited the doll exchange on the Sunday. That is a considerable number, taking New Zealand's small population and the long distances into consideration. Here too a Hildegard Günzel doll was awarded a „Gold". During this trip a small teddy bear caused additional commotion. His name was „Benjamin" and belonged to Carol Stanton,

Elise, 1996, limitiert je 35 Exemplare Europa/USA, gewann den Doll of Excellence, Dolls Magazin, USA.

Elise, 1996, production limited to 35 samples each Europe/USA, won the Doll of Excellence, Dolls Magazin USA.

Das Jahr 1987 kennzeichneten mehrere Veränderungen im Leben Hildegard Günzels. In diesem Jahr schuf sie die letzte Form für Wanke. Sie leitete damals auch mehrere Seminare für Astry Campbell, die erkrankt war. Hildegard Günzel war ja die zweite Seminarleiterin - nach Astry Campbell - in Deutschland. Und sie verfaßte ein Buch, das Wegbereiter für die dritte Generation Künstlerpuppenmacher werden sollte: „Künstlerpuppen selbermachen". Das Buch erschien zunächst in deutscher Sprache im Verlag „Laterna magica" des Verleger- und Puppensammler-Ehepaares Richter in München. Es war weltweit ein großer Erfolg und wurde in vier Sprachen übersetzt. In USA erreichte es Platz vier der Bestsellerliste von Hobby House Press. Hildegard Günzel: „Die Zeit war damals einfach reif für ein solches Buch. Puppenmachen war inzwischen zu einem weit verbreiteten Hobby

who always carried him with her on all her trips. Benjamin was only 10 cm tall, but for this decidedly adventurous. On more than one occasion Carol Stanton lamented about the supposed loss of her teddy bear. She firmly resolved to look after him - in vain. Finally she packed him away into her toilet bag, which she always had on her in her hand luggage in the aeroplane. The return flight in those days stopped in Singapore. All three, Hildegard Günzel, Carol Stanton, and Matthias Wanke sauntered through the airport terminal and had a look in this and the other shop. Then, as they were alighting the aircraft, Carol froze. The toilet bag was gone! And even worse, Benjamin was gone! She turned round on the stairs. Matthias Wanke grabbed her by the arm and ran back with her all the way into the departure hall. She actually found both bag and bear again in a Duty Free Shop. In the

geworden, doch oftmals verfügten die Autodidakten in Sachen Puppen nicht über die erforderlichen anatomischen Kenntnisse. Und nicht alle waren in der Lage, Kurse und Seminare zu besuchen. Mit diesem Buch konnte nun jeder, der sich berufen fühlte, Puppen zu machen, zu Hause ungestört lernen und arbeiten". Viele der heute bekannten Puppenmacher bezogen ihre Kenntnisse aus diesem Buch. Es ist inzwischen ein „Klassiker", trotzdem denkt Hildegard Günzel daran, ein neues herauszugeben, das von Anfang an zweisprachig erscheinen soll.

In diesem Jahr, 1987, gab es auch eine Revolution auf dem Puppenmarkt: Annette Himstedt stellte auf der Nürnberger Spielwarenmesse ihre ersten Puppen aus Vinyl vor. Eine neue Ära des Puppensammelns begann, denn nun konnten sich auch solche Menschen Künstlerpuppen leisten, denen die „Originale" aus Porzellan zu teuer waren. Natürlich war auch Matthias Wanke von dieser Idee spontan begeistert. Auch Hildegard Günzel hatte schon „lange über etwas Derartiges nachgedacht". Da trat eine deutsche Firma mit Anfragen an sie heran, ob sie nicht auch Vinylpuppen entwerfen wollte. Daraufhin entschloß sich Matthias Wanke schnell zu einer eigenen Vinyl-Serie. Die Firma „Classic Children" wurde extra dafür gegründet, und Hildegard Günzel erhielt den Auftrag, Modelle zu entwerfen. Die erste Kollektion wurde 1988 auf den Spielwarenmessen in Nürnberg und New York vorgestellt und vom Publikum begeistert aufgenommen. In diesem Jahr erzielte die Künstlerin den Doty Award für die „Classic"-Puppe „Doris."
Die Puppen der Firma „Classic Children" wurden jedoch nicht in Deutschland, sondern in China gefertigt, und es war infolge der Verständigungsprobleme nicht immer leicht, den gewünschten Qualitätsstandard zu erreichen.
Seit ihrer ersten Toy Fair wird Hildegard Günzel in jedem Jahr zu allen großen Messen in USA eingeladen.

Gaylord, 1996, limitiert je 35 Exemplare Europa/USA.
Gaylord, 1996 production limited to 35 samples each for Europe/USA.

Lara, 1996, limitiert je 35 Exemplare Europa/USA (links).
Lara 1996, production limited to 35 samples each for Europe/USA.

79

Bei einem ihrer ersten Besuche in Disneyworld, Orlando, saß sie eines Abends zusammen mit Pat Thompson und Elke Hutchem an der Bar. Sie hatte Fotos ihrer Puppen dabei, die sie ihren beiden Kolleginnen zeigte. Ihre Agentin kam vorbei in Begleitung von zwei Herren. Hildegard Günzel lud sie ein, Platz zu nehmen. Einer der Herren warf einen Blick auf die Fotos und fragte: „Wer hat diese Puppen gemacht?" Bevor er ging, verabredete er mit der Künstlerin ein Treffen für den nächsten Morgen. Da stellte sich dann heraus, daß er einer der Inhaber einer großen amerikanischen Puppenfirma war, und zwar der Alexander Doll Company, eines der traditionsreichsten und exklusivsten Häuser. Mr. Ira Smith und der Vizepräsident, Beau James, hatten am Vorabend mit Hildegard Günzel an der Bar gesessen. Diese Begegnung war ein weiterer Meilenstein in ihrer Karriere. Erst zwei Jahre zuvor hatte „Madame Alexander" die Firma an die jetzigen Inhaber verkauft. Nun war man an neuen Modellen interessiert und fragte Hildegard Günzel, ob sie nicht bei der Alexander Doll Company einen Vertrag unterzeichnen wolle.

Die Nürnberger Spielwarenmesse findet traditionell in der ersten Februarwoche statt. Sie ist eine der größten Spielwarenmessen der Welt und mit Sicherheit die größte Europas. Die Wartelisten für Aussteller sind lang. Im Normalfall braucht man mehrere Jahre, bis man einen Stand erhält. 1990 hatte Hildegard Günzel erstmalig einen eigenen Stand. „Ich dachte, Ostern und Weihnachten fallen zusammen!" Erst später wurde ihr klar, daß sie seit langem - unbewußt, „aus dem Bauch heraus" - die Selbständigkeit, eine eigene Firma, angestrebt hatte. Es hatte nur so lange gedauert, weil sie ihre Freiheit nicht aufgeben wollte. Zwar hatte sie schon früher „Puppenhäuser" und Mitarbeiter, doch: „Irgendwie waren das immer noch Spielwiesen für mich gewesen. Ich leistete mir zwar schon manchmal eine Anzeige in einer Fachzeitschrift, hatte aber noch nicht so recht begriffen, wie wichtig

meanwhile under the disapproving glance of the air stewardess, Hildegard Günzel stood with one foot in the aircraft and the other firmly outside, and was firmly resolved to prevent the aircraft from taking off until all were back. Whereupon Carol Stanton decided to leave the impudent teddy at home in the future. Hildegard Günzel, together with Astry Campbell, had already declared that for the 4th international G.D.S. competition on 18.10.1996 in Salzburg, the town in which Mozart lived, that they would check the artistic dolls upon submission to verify that no prefabricated parts had been used which were available through the trade, such as plastic masks for soft dolls or doll's limbs made from commercially available casts. In the meantime the terms and conditions of the competition had become stricter than they had been at the beginning. Now every doll, including head, arms, and legs, had to be created by the artist themselves. At that time it was still normal for all doll artists to produce so called „Vario" series of dolls. A single cast was made and different dolls manufactured from it. The mouth of a doll, which otherwise had closed lips, was opened, the recess for the eyes was either enlarged or reduced and often the same hands and feet, which for this reason were more stylised and less characteristic, were used for different dolls. However the rules became even more strict and the standards even higher. Precisely this is also thanks to Hildegard Günzel, for often innovations in the sphere of artistic dolls are associated with the name Günzel. Many have benefited from this, both doll-makers and doll-collectors. So it was that in 1985 she was the first doll's artist to model dolls with bended legs with knees shaped in the cast. As a result her dolls became even more „flexible". Now they had one leg for support and one which could be moved, which makes graceful poses just as easy as sitting. Hildegard Günzel had herself gone to ballet classes for ten years. The knowledge acquired in those days now influenced her

Werbung für mich ist. Ich habe das damals alles noch nicht so ernst genommen. Ich bin nun mal verspielt. Geschäftliches hatte immer etwas Anrüchiges für mich. Vielleicht kommt das daher, daß ich aus einem Lehrerhaushalt stamme. Ich war Künstlerin und wollte es bleiben. - Eigentlich war das ziemlich arrogant". Diese erste Nürnberger Messe war ein großer Erfolg. Allerdings hatte sich Hildegard Günzel auch gut darauf vorbereitet. „Damals," erzählte sie, „war mein erster Gang zur Bank. Sonst hatte ich meine Geschäfte immer über den Daumen kalkuliert. In den ersten Jahren konnte man das noch machen. Doch jetzt - im internationalen Geschäft - ging das nicht mehr. Dieser Markt ist hart!"

Die Nachricht von M. Wankes Tod war ein schwerer Schock für sie. Denn: „Ich verlor mit ihm einen loyalen Freund." Niemand konnte es fassen. Die Puppenwelt war um eine faszi-

work. Shortly afterwards, dolls in a sitting position with a bended knee could be seen from other lady doll-makers. Hildegard Günzel thinks it is a good thing that many others in the doll world are inspired by her work. If a new pose - in 1991 it was using hands as a prop which she introduced - have been imitated by other doll artists for their dolls, she takes it as a compliment for her work. She is open towards others and approachable, shares her experiences with them and is not afraid either to learn from others. Competition is important. Those that do take their competition seriously, are paying them respect. Petty jealousies are not Hildegard Günzel's way. She says, "I am addicted to harmony. Best of all I would like to be loved by everyone". Hildegard Günzel is a professional, but first of all she had to learn about marketing. At that time, in 1986, she enjoyed being

Der Malplatz der Künstlerin. Jedes Gesicht wird von ihr eigenhändig bemalt.

The artist's painting desk. Each face is painted by her personally.

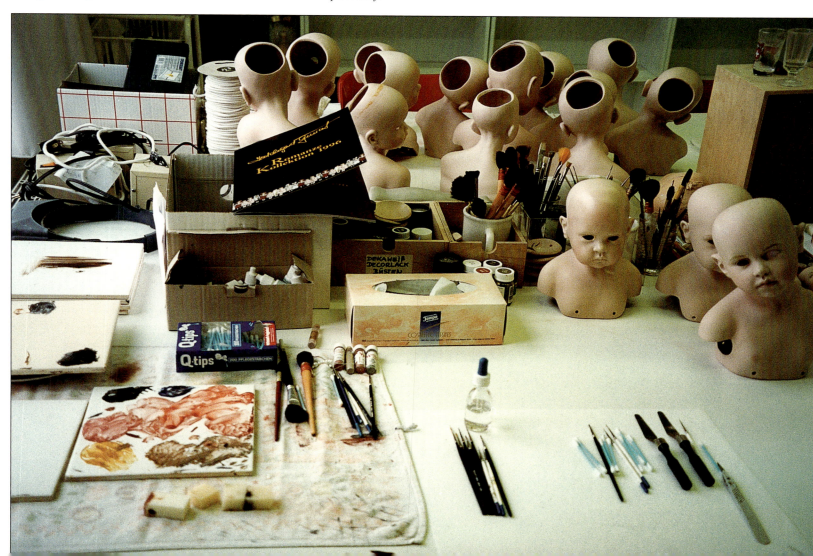

nierende Gestalt ärmer geworden. Zwar erbte Ruth Grau, die Mutter von Matthias Wanke, das Unternehmen und führte es auch noch einige Jahre in seinem Sinne weiter, bis es 1995 an die Firma Glorex verkauft wurde, doch für Hildegard Günzel stand fest, daß sie sich von der Firma Wanke trennen würde. Leicht fiel es ihr nicht - nach so vielen Jahren des gemeinsamen Aufbaus.

1989 war ein trauriges Jahr. Hildegard Günzel fühlte, daß sich ihr künstlerischer Weg erneut ändern würde. Wohin würde er sie führen?

1990 unterschrieb Hildegard Günzel einen Vertrag mit der Alexander Doll Company für eine Vinyl-Serie. Auf der Toy Fair in New York stellte sie im Show-Room von Alexander aus, und die Puppen der „Hildegard-Günzel-Collection" wurden ganzjährig im Fenster des Toy Buildings auf der 5th Avenue präsentiert. Alexander feierte eine neue Hildegard Günzel. Jedes Jahr veranstaltete die Firma eine Promotionstour für sie durch mehrere Staaten und Städte der USA, die Camille Kahn, ihre Betreuerin in der „Collection", für sie organisierte. Hildegard Günzel lernte Amerika und die Amerikaner kennen und schätzen. Zum einen, weil sie offen und unkompliziert sind und sich ihr gegenüber immer als gute Kollegen erwiesen haben. Ein kleinlicher Konkurrenzgeist existiert dort nicht; alle geben auf Fragen nach ihren Erfahrungen und Arbeitsmethoden gern und bereitwillig Auskunft. Trotzdem ist der Markt dort hart, härter als in Europa. Ausländischen Puppenkünstlerinnen fällt es oft schwer, dort Fuß zu fassen. Hildegard Günzel rät deshalb jedem, bevor er den Entschluß faßt, nach USA zu gehen, erst einmal den eigenen, heimischen Markt zu erobern. Sie selbst hat viele gute Freunde in den USA gefunden - genau wie ihre Puppen: 1990 wurde eine ihrer Puppen „Tricia" mit dem „Doll of Excellence" des Doll Magazin ausgezeichnet, drei Nominationen und den „Doty Award" erhielt sie ebenfalls in diesem Jahr. 1991 waren es vier Nominationen, und zweimal gab es den

allowed to get to know the world for once. She was as astonished as a child and was as pleased as Punch that so many people from all different nationalities, loved her dolls. The precondition for this was for people from different nationalities 'to have the same eye'. There are manifestly no differences between the nationalities; whether American, Japanese, or German, all doll lovers have the same eye. If Hildegard Günzel saw that a woman had this eye, she always tried to help her obtain the coveted doll. The first journey to New York has remained unforgettable for her. Matthias Wanke had suggested to her that she take three dolls with her to New York, he said he knew someone who would be prepared to show the dolls on their stand. „When I was sitting down at breakfast and saw how large the city is, I thought, „You're crazy"! But the Americans are very straightforward". Hildegard Günzel quickly made contact with doll-makers and collectors who for their part introduced her amongst their circle of acquaintances. After three hours everybody at the exhibition knew who Hildegard Günzel was. In 1986 she was awarded the „Doty Award" by „Doll Reader" for „Cinderella". And just the same thing happened to her as had done with „Marion" two years previously. Again it resulted in a copyright-conflict. Walt Disney made it clear in friendly but no uncertain terms, that the name „Cinderella" was protected by copyright and therefore out of bounds for everyone else. The doll had to be renamed and was then simply called „Milk Maid". Nevertheless New York turned out to be a great success. The Günzel-Doll-boom in the USA began with The 'Doty Award' by „Doll Reader" and the awarding of „Doll of Excellence" by the „Doll Magazine". Matthias Wanke and Hildegard Günzel returned home with new orders in the bag. But where could she obtain the money to finance all these orders? Doing business in the USA is quite different from doing business in Europe. American collectors attach importance to

Anläßlich der Eröffnung des Puppenmuseums, hier mit Produktionsleiterin Doris Tessendorf.
On the occasion of the opening of the doll museum, here with the production manageress Doris Tessendorf.

„Doty Award", je einen für „Iris" und „Melody with friend" und eine Nomination „Doll of Excellence".
1992 errang „Courtney" den „Doll of Excellence". In diesem Jahr kam Frank Wohlfarth, Verleger und Herausgeber der deutschen Puppenfachzeitschrift „Puppen & Spielzeug" zu ihr und sagte: „Frau Günzel, Sie müssen mehr werben!" Bis dahin hatte sie nur hier und da einmal eine Anzeige. Nun schaltete sie vier Anzeigen in „Puppen & Spielzeug" und im nächsten Jahr doppelt so viele, denn ihr Umsatz hatte sich verdoppelt! Sie hatte erkannt,

receiving a doll exactly as ordered. „What you see is what you get !" Unlike Germany, where collectors endeavour to obtain as individual a piece as possible and tolerate minor deviations in colour and quality of material, this sort of thing would be out of the question in the USA. If a doll is limited to a run of 70 models, it must also be guaranteed that there is sufficient material of the same quality available for all dolls. Obviously such quantities cannot simply be bought from the shop round the corner. Today Hildegard Günzel buys in directly from the manufacturers and places orders on the condition that she must be able to place follow-up orders, at any time, for the same material in the same quality. At that time, in 1986 she wasn't so far advanced and for this reason „Cinderella" renamed as „Milk Maid" was clothed in different materials. Now the Günzel dolls moved into a larger studio. The new „House of Dolls" had 200 m2 of floor space on two floors. Casts were shored in the four production rooms on the ground floor, where they were cast, cleaned and fired. The finishing room, office, and exhibition rooms were on the upper floor. In 1986 Günzel dolls were shown at exhibitions in Tokyo, Australia, and New Zealand in addition to Germany and the USA. 1987 saw several changes in Hildegard Günzel's life. In the course of this year she made her last cast for the Wanke company. And she took over several seminars for Astry Campbell, who had fallen ill. Hildegard Günzel was indeed the number two seminar leader in Germany - after Astry Campbell. And she published a book which was supposed to prepare the way for the third generation of artist doll-makers. „Making artistic dolls yourself" First of all the book appeared in German from the „Laterna magica" publishing house managed by the Richters, a couple from Munich who were both publishers and doll-collectors. It was a large success world-wide and was translated into four languages. In the USA it reached fourth place in the best seller list from the

wie wichtig Marketing ist und rät jedem Puppenkünstler, mehr in das Marketing zu investieren. Hildegard Günzel hat in diesem Jahr auch ein weiteres Buch veröffentlicht, „Puppenträume". Herausgeber ist Frank Wohlfarth. Die Arbeit an „Puppenträume" hat Hildegard Günzel jedoch noch in anderer Hinsicht Glück gebracht: Sie ist inzwischen mit Frank Wohlfarth verheiratet!

Ende 1993 war ihr klar, daß sie ihr „Puppenhaus" in Süddeutschland aufgeben und in den „Norden", nach Duisburg, wo Frank Wohlfarth zu Hause ist, ziehen würde. Und es war ihr auch klar, daß sie ihr eigenes Unternehmen weiter ausbauen wollte. Längst war das alte „Puppenhaus" zu klein geworden. Nun wurden „Nägel mit Köpfen" gemacht, und die Fabrikationsstätte der „Puppenmanufaktur Hildegard Günzel" wurde gebaut. Ihre Puppenkinder hatten endlich ein ihnen angemessenes Domizil!

May, 1996, limitiert je 35 Exemplare Europa/USA.
May, 1996, production limited to 35 samples each for Europe/USA.

Hobby House Press. About this Hildegard Günzel said „Then the time was simply ripe for such a book. In the meantime doll-making had become a very widespread hobby, but often the self-taught in doll making didn't possess the anatomical knowledge necessary. And not all were in a position to take part in courses and seminars. Now, anyone who felt called to make dolls could learn and work at home in peace and quiet with the aid of this book". „Many of the doll-makers well known today drew their knowledge from this book. In the meantime it has become a „classic". Nevertheless Hildegard Günzel is thinking of publishing a new one which is to be bi-lingual from the outset. In 1987 a revolution took place in the dolls' market : Annette Himstedt exhibited her first dolls made of vinyl at the Nuremberg Toy Fair. A new era in doll-collecting began, for now even those people for whom the „Originals" made of porcelain were too expensive could afford artistic dolls. Of course, Matthias Wanke was spontaneously enthusiastic about this idea. Even Hildegard Günzel had already been thinking along similar lines for a long time. Then in Nuremberg a Germany company approached her with an enquiry as to whether she would like to manufacture vinyl dolls as well. Whereupon Matthias Wanke quickly decided to make his own vinyl series. „Classic Children" company was especially established for this purpose, and an order was placed with Hildegard Günzel to design models. The first collection was presented in the toy fairs in Nuremberg and New York in 1988 and was enthusiastically received by the public. In the same year Hildegard Günzel was awarded the „Doty Award" for the „Classic" doll „Doris". In the following year in Disney World in Orlando, „Marissa" was elected as the „Doll of Excellence". In 1990 „Tricia" won the „Doll of Excellence" award. However the dolls were not manufactured in China, but in Germany, and it was not always easy to achieve the standards of quality desired as a result of the communication barrier. Since

Madeleine, 1996, Entwurf für die G.D.S. Schule in Duisburg.
Madelaine, 1996, draft for the G.D.S. school in Duisburg.

her first toy fair, Hildegard Günzel has been invited to all the large toy fairs in the USA. During one of her first visits to Disney World in Orlando, she was sitting in the bar one evening together with Pat Thompson and Elke Hutchem. She had photographs of her dolls with her, which she was showing to both her colleagues. Her agent came up to them, accompanied by two men. Hildegard Günzel invited them to take a seat. One of the men cast a glance at the photographs and asked, „Who made these dolls?" Before he left, he had agreed a meeting for the following morning with Hildegard Günzel. Then it turned out that he was one of the owners of a large American doll company, the Alexander Doll Company in fact one of the most traditional and exclusive firms. Mr. Ira Smith and the Vice President Beau James had been sitting in the bar with Hildegard Günzel on the previous evening. This meeting was another milestone in her career. Only two years previously „Madame Alexander" had sold the company to its present owner. Now they were interested in new models and asked Hildegard Günzel whether she wouldn't like to sign a contract with the Alexander Doll Company. The Nuremberg Toy Fair is traditionally held in the first week in February. It is one of the biggest toy fairs in the world and certainly the biggest in Europe. The waiting lists for exhibitors is long. Normally it takes several years to be offered a stand. In 1990 Hildegard Günzel had her own stand for the first time. „It felt as if birthday and Christmas had been rolled into one". Only later did it become clear to her that for a long time - unconsciously from deep inside - had been striving towards independence, to running her own company. It had only taken so long because she had harboured no wish to relinquish her freedom. „Admittedly, she had already had „Houses of Dolls" and staff, but „somehow they had still been a playground for me". I had indeed been able to afford an occasional advertisement in the trade press but I still hadn't really under-

Samantha, Jubiläumspuppe, 1997, limitiert 25 Exemplare weltweit.
Samantha, jubilee doll 1997, production limited to 25 samples world-wide.

stood how important advertising is for me. At that time I still didn't take everything very seriously. I'm just playful. Business had always been disreputable as far as I was concerned. Perhaps the reason for this is that I came from a family of teachers. I was an artist and wanted to remain one. Actually that was a fairly arrogant attitude" (Günzel). This first Nuremberg Toy Fair was a great success. Admittedly Hildegard Günzel was well prepared for it. „At that time", she says „My first trip was to the bank. Before that I had always run my affairs with rough calculations. It was possible to do that in the early years. But now - in international business - this was no longer possible. This is a tough market !" M. Wanke´s the news of his death was a heavy blow for her. „For with him I lost a faithful friend". Nobody could take it in. The doll's world had become poorer with the loss of a fascinating personality. Admittedly Ruth Grau, the mother of Matthias Wanke, inherited the company and also continued to manage it for some years as he would have wished, until it was sold 1995 to the Glorex company. But one thing was certain for Hildegard Günzel, that she would part company with the Wanke Company. It wasn't easy for her - after so many years of building up together. 1989 was a sad year. Hildegard Günzel felt that her artistic path would take another direction again. Where would it lead her? In 1990 Hildegard Günzel signed a contract with the Alexander Doll Company for a vinyl series. At the Toy Fair in New York she exhibited in a show room within the Alexander stand and the dolls of the „Hildegard Günzel collection" were shown all year round in the display window of the Toy Building on 5th Avenue. Alexander were celebrating a new Hildegard Günzel. Every year the company organised a promotional tour for her through several states and cities of the USA, which Camille Kahn, Hildegard Günzel's member of staff in the „Collection", organised for her. Hildegard Günzel got to know and value America and the Americans.

Imogene, 1997, limitiert je 25 Exemplare
Europa/USA.
*Imogene, 1997, production limited to 25 samples each
for Europe/USA.*

On the one hand because they are open and straightforward, and have always turned out to be good colleagues to her. A spirit of petty competitiveness doesn't exist over there, everyone is happy and willing to provide information in response to questions regarding their experience and methods of working. For all that, the market over there is hard, harder than in Europe. It is often difficult for foreign makers of artistic dolls to establish themselves. For this reason Hildegard Günzel would advise everyone to first of all conquer their own domestic market before taking the decision to go to the USA. Hildegard Günzel has made many good friends in the USA - just as her dolls have done. In 1990 one of her dolls, „Tricia", was nominated the „Doll of Excellence" by the „Doll Magazine", she also received three nominations the „Doty Award" in the same year. In 1991 it was four nominations and the „Doty Award" twice, once each for „Iris" and „Melody with Friend" and one „Doll of Excellence" nomination. In 1992 „Courtney" was nominated „Doll of Excellence". In the same year Frank Wohlfarth, publisher and editor of the German specialist journal for dolls „Puppen & Spielzeug" approached her and said, „Mrs. Günzel, you must advertise more!" Up until then Hildegard Günzel had only placed an advertisement here and there. Now she placed four adverts in „Puppen & Spielzeug" and in the following year twice as many again, because her turnover had doubled. She had recognised how important marketing is and advises every doll artist to invest more in marketing. In the same year Hildegard Günzel also published another book „Dolls' Dreams", published by Frank Wohlfarth. However the work on „Dolls' Dreams" brought Hildegard Günzel happiness in another respect as well. In the meantime she has married Frank Wohlfarth. At the end of 1993 it was obvious to her that she would have to give up her „ House of Dolls „ in southern Germany and move up „North" to Duisburg where Frank

Wohlfarth has his home. And it was also clear to hear that she wanted to expand her own business further. The old „ House of Dolls „ had been too small for her for a long time. Now things were not going to be done by halves and the workshop premises of „Puppenmanufaktur Hildegard Günzel" were built. Her doll-children had a home fit for them at last.

Harriet mit Daisy und Buttercup, 1997, limitiert je 25 Exemplare Europa/USA.
Harriet with Daisy and Buttercup, 1997, production limited to 25 samples each for Europe/USA.

Vom „Schneckenhaus" hinaus in die Welt
Out from the snail's shell into the world

Von außen ist dem Gebäude, in dem die Gün-zel-Puppen entstehen, nicht anzusehen, wel-che Überraschungen sich in seinem Inneren verbergen. Die Fassade ist eher schlicht und zweckmäßig. Dem Besucher, der es durch die breite Glastür betritt, öffnet sich dahinter je-doch eine zwar luftig helle und freundliche, dennoch nicht weniger zauberhafte, magische Welt: Er befindet sich im Museum der Gün-zel-Puppen. Wie eine Schnecke konzipiert ist dieser Teil des Gebäudes, das den zweiten Preis für Industrie-Design des Landes Nordrhein-Westfalen erhielt. Von allen Seiten flutet Licht in die Räume, auch von oben. Dadurch ist ei-ne optimale Präsentation der Puppen gewähr-leistet, ohne störende Schatten. In Linkswin-dungen führt der Gang den Besucher an Vitri-nen und Mauerdurchbrüchen vorbei, in de-nen Puppen stehen. Er verfolgt den Werde-gang Hildegard Günzels. Außer Unikaten, die von Anfang an für ein Museum gedacht wa-ren, findet je eine Puppe aus der jährlichen Kollektion hier ihren Platz, auch die Modell-köpfe für Günzel-Puppen aus Vinyl, die seit 1994 in Zusammenarbeit mit der Waltershäu-ser Puppenmanufaktur entstehen. Wer hier je-doch eine genaue chronologische Abfolge und ein nüchternes, „museumsmäßiges" Aneinan-derreihen von Puppen erwartet, wird ange-nehm enttäuscht. In Theaterbühnen nach-empfundenen Szenenbildern findet man „märchenhafte" Darstellungen. Fasziniert sieht sich der Besucher mit den Mythen und Traumbildern seiner eigenen Kindheit kon-frontiert. Nicht nur der deutsche. Heute steht uns der Märchen- und Mythenschatz aller eu-ropäischen Völker zur Verfügung, und wir entdecken, daß sie alle ähnlich sind. Es sind Urbilder der Menschenseele selbst, die in Worte gefaßt und auf diese Weise überliefert wurden. Es ist der Schatz des Abendlandes, je-dem zugänglich, der die Formel kennt, ihn zu

The exterior of the building in which the Günzel dolls are created gives not the slightest indication of the surprises concealed inside. The facade is rather plain and functional. To the visitor who enters the wide glass doors, there opens up however an environment which is airy, light, and friendly, but is nevert-heless no less an enchanting and magical world. The visitor finds himself in the Günzel dolls' museum. This section of the building has been designed in the form of a snail, and was awarded second prize for Industrial Design in the North Rhine-Westphalia regi-on. Light floods into the room from all sides, directly from above too. As a result this gua-rantees an optimal presentation of the dolls, without the interference of shadows. The cor-ridor leads the visitor in a left turn past show cases and display sections set into the walls, in which dolls are displayed. They represent the career development of Hildegard Günzel. With the exception of unicums, which from the outset were conceived for a museum, there is a place for each doll from the annual collec-tion here, even the model heads for Günzel dolls made of vinyl which have been created in co-operation with the Waltershäuser doll-making company since 1994. Those visitors who nevertheless expect an exact chronologi-cal sequence and the sober „pedestrian" lining up of dolls next to each other as you would find in a museum will be pleasantly disap-pointed. You will find „fairy-tale like" presen-tations in settings modelled on theatre stages. Fascinated, visitors see themselves confronted with the myths and dream-images of their own childhood. And not only German visi-tors. Today we have the rich store of fairy tales and myths of all European peoples at our dis-posal, and we have discovered that they are all similar. They are archetypes of the human soul itself, couched in words and handed down

Samantha, Portrait
der Jubiläumspuppe.
*Samantha, portrait of
the anniversary doll.*

90

heben. Puppenmacher - Menschen - wie Hildegard Günzel gehören zu diesen Privilegierten. Sie bedienen sich dieser Bilder oft bei ihrer Arbeit. Ob Lady Genoveva, Lady Marian und Alice im Wunderland - oder Schneewittchen und die sieben Zwerge - sie alle hat die Künstlerin schon umgesetzt. In einer Szene aus Goethes „Faust" beugt sich ein beeindruckender, dämonischer Mephisto über ein zartes „Gretchen", und im innersten Raum, dem Kern der Schnecke, entdeckt man die Elfenkönigin zu Pferde, umgeben von ihrem Hofstaat, bestehend aus skurrilen Wald- und Erdgeistern. In den in rauchgrauen Tönen gehaltenen Trompe d´oil-Malereien der Laffitten und Kulissen entdeckt man originelle Details: Die gemalten Putten, die die seitlich gerafften Vorhänge halten, sind keine Putten im herkömmlichen Sinn. Es sind eindeutig Babypuppen, bei denen man die Befestigung der modellierten Gliedmaßen am „Stoff"körper erkennen kann.

Zuerst hatte Hildegard Günzel beabsichtigt, die Wände dieser Räume schwarz ausmalen zu lassen, wodurch eine geheimnisvolle Atmosphäre entstanden wäre. Die beleuchteten Szenen hätten so noch mehr Theaterbühnen geglichen. Heute ist sie froh, davon Abstand genommen zu haben, denn das Museum wurde ja nicht eingerichtet, um Besucher zu beeindrucken, sondern um sie auf ansprechende Weise mit den verschiedenen Aspekten von Hildegard Günzels Arbeit vertraut zu machen. Oft besuchen andere Puppenmacher das Museum, die hier auch herzlich willkommen sind. So ist das Museum auch eine interessante Begegnungsstätte vieler Puppenkünstler. Exklusiv für G.D.S. Mitglieder hat sie auf der Galerie ihres Museums einen Raum geschaffen, in dem sie Modellier-Seminare abhält, „Die Puppenmacher-Masterclass" wurde 1995 ins Leben gerufen. Nur Drei-Sterne-Lehrer bilden hier aus. Ja, die Puppendesignerin ist der G.D.S. bis heute treu geblieben. Sie hat nicht vergessen, was sie dieser weltweiten Vereini-

orally. This is the treasure of the occident, accessible to all who know how to raise it. Doll makers - people - like Hildegard Günzel rank amongst the privileged. They often avail themselves of these images in their work. Whether Lady Genoveva, Lady Marian and Alice in Wonderland - or Snow White and the Seven Dwarfs - Hildegard Günzel has already created them all. In a scene from Goethes „Faust" an impressive „demonic Mephistopheles" leans over a tender „Gretchen". In the innermost room forming the centre of the volute, one can discover the elfin queen on horseback, surrounded by her royal train, consisting of bizarre woodland and earth spirits. Original details can be discovered in the „Trompe d'oeil" paintings of the settings and scenery which are restrained in smoke-grey hues. The painted puttos which hold the curtains gathered up to the side are not puttos in the traditional sense. They are unmistakable baby dolls on which the fitting of the modelled limbs to the material torso can be seen. First of all Hildegard Günzel had intended to have the walls of this abstract painted black, thereby creating a mysterious atmosphere. The illuminated scenes would have resembled theatre stages all the more. Today she is glad that she looked at things in their proper perspective, since the museum wasn't established to impress visitors after all, but to familiarise them with the different aspects of Hildegard Günzel's work in an appropriate manner which would appeal to them. Other dollmakers often visit the museum and they are also extended a warm welcome. This is how the museum has become an interesting meeting place for many doll artists. She has created a room in the gallery of the museum in which she holds modelling seminars exclusively for G.D.S. members. „The Doll Makers" master class was set up and started in 1995. Only three-star teachers lecture here. Yes, Hildegard Günzel has remained faithful to the G.D.S. to this today. She has not forgotten what she owes this world-wide association and

gung zu verdanken hat und hat den Wunsch, sie weiterhin zu unterstützen, denn: „Es gibt keine Konkurrenz der Lehrer untereinander, es steht kein kommerzielles Interesse dahinter. Die G.D.S. verpflichtet niemanden, mit bestimmten Firmen zusammenzuarbeiten. Und: Fast alle heutigen Puppenmacher haben mit ihr angefangen".

Einen reizvollen und eigentümlich sphärischen Anblick bietet die zum Seminarraum hinauf führende Treppe mit Stufen aus durchsichtigem, grünlichem Acrylglas. Wie eine Leiter aus blitzenden Lichtstreifen wirkt sie von unten. Von oben sieht es aus, als sprängen Fluten türkisfarbenen Wassers kaskadenförmig hinab. Die Arbeitstische aus Massivholz sind ringförmig um das Innere des Schneckenhauses angeordnet. Die Kursteilnehmer, die sich nach vorn beugen und wie in einen Schacht nach unten schauen, können dort die Elfenkönigin und ihr Gefolge erblicken und sich von ihr inspirieren lassen. Fünf Tage dauert ein Kursus, in dessen Verlauf den Teilnehmern alle Kenntnisse vermittelt werden, die sie benötigen, um eine eigene Puppe zu modellieren. Nicht nur Köpfe entstehen dabei, sondern auch die Brustplatte, Arme und Beine.

Im hinteren Teil des Gebäudes ist die Manufaktur untergebracht. Hier werden die fertigen Puppen bekleidet, hier modelliert Hildegard Günzel, hier werden Formen ausgegossen, Rohlinge versäubert, gebrannt, bemalt, erneut gebrannt und schließlich gewachst. Auch wenn dieser letzte Arbeitsgang, den heute nur noch ganz wenige Puppenmacher beibehalten haben, den Zeitrahmen, den eine Puppe bis zur Fertigstellung beansprucht, enorm vergrößert, geht die Künstlerin von dieser Besonderheit nicht ab. Nicht zuletzt durch diesen abschließenden hauchzarten Überzug erhalten ihre Puppen den berühmten „touch", den Sammler weltweit an ihren Puppen so lieben.

wishes to continue supporting it since, „There is no competition amongst the teachers, there is no hidden commercial interest. The G.D.S. doesn't oblige anyone to work together with specific companies. And, almost all present day doll-makers started out with it „. The steps leading up to the seminar room, with its treads made of transparent, greenish, acrylic glass offer a charming and in fact spherical view. From below it looks like a flashing beam of light. From above it seems like torrents of turquoise-coloured water cascading downwards. The work tables are made of solid wood and are arranged in a circle around the volute. The course participants who lean forward and look down the quasi shaft can catch sight of the elfin queen and her retinue and can allow themselves to be inspired by her. A course lasts five days, during which time the participants are taught all the knowledge and skills they need to model their own doll. Not only heads are made, but also the breast plate, arms and legs. The production room is accommodated in the rear section of the building. Here the completed dolls are clothed. This is where Hildegard Günzel models and where casts are made, castings are cleaned off, fired, painted, given a secondary firing and finally waxed. Even if this last stage in the process which has still been retained by only a few doll-makers is extremely time consuming and lengthens the time required to make a doll considerably, Hildegard Günzel insists upon this special element of the manufacturing process. Not least because with this final wafer-thin coating her dolls are given the famous „touch" which collectors world-wide love so much about her dolls. Hildegard Günzel's staff all work for her on a permanent basis. She rebuilt her team in 1994. Her colleague and friend of many years, Uschi Creyels, made a large contribution to this restructuring and lived with her and Frank Wohlfarth in their Duisburg home for several months. All staff work independently. Inspite of this each individual doll is made by Hildegard Günzel. She

Miss Camille mit Smoothy and The Duchess of Catsfield, 1997, limitiert10 Exemplare.

Miss Camille with Smoothy and The Duchess of Catsfield, 1997, production limited to 10 samples.

Hildegard Günzels Mitarbeiterinnen sind alle fest angestellt. Sie hat dieses Team 1994 neu aufgebaut. Dazu hat Uschi Creyels, ihre langjährige Mitarbeiterin und Freundin,einen großen Teil beigetragen und einige Monate im Duisburger Haushalt mitgelebt. Alle arbeiten völlig selbständig. Trotzdem ist jede einzelne Puppe eine von Hildegard Günzel gefertigte Puppe. Sie schleift Köpfe, öffnet Augenausschnitte, und natürlich bemalt sie alle Puppen selbst. Alle Porzellanpuppen, die die Manufaktur verlassen, werden mit der gleichen Sorgfalt hergestellt. Dazu fühlt sich Hildegard Günzel

smoothes heads, widens eye sockets, and of course she paints all dolls herself. All porcelain dolls which pass through the production process are manufactured with the same care. Hildegard Günzel feels obliged to ensure this not only for the sake of her business partners and collectors, but also for the sake of her staff. In the meantime she has come to fully regard herself as an entrepreneur. This isn't always easy. You can deal with anything that doesn't concern other people in a relaxed manner. As an artist, but also as a business woman, you sometimes overlook the fact that every

nicht nur ihren Geschäftspartnern und Sammlern gegenüber verpflichtet, sondern auch ihren Mitarbeiterinnen. Inzwischen steht sie voll dazu, Unternehmerin zu sein. „Das ist nicht immer leicht. Man kann alle Dinge locker angehen, die nicht andere Menschen betreffen. Als Künstlerin, aber auch als Unternehmer, denkt man manchmal nicht daran, daß alle Entscheidungen, die man trifft, auch andere mit treffen, und daß Mitarbeiter nicht automatisch die gleichen Ideale haben, wie man selbst. Deshalb möchte ich, daß es in unserer Firma familiär zugeht. Wenn alle Mitarbeiter mich mögen, dann kann ich sie auch motivieren, dann lassen sie sich von meiner Begeisterung anstecken". Manchmal funktioniert das auch umgekehrt. Teamgeist wird groß geschrieben im Haus der Günzel-Puppen, denn alle wissen, daß sie einander brauchen, um sie entstehen zu lassen.

Deshalb sind heute lange Vorbereitungen nötig, bis eine neue Kollektion fertig ist. Zuerst findet Hildegard Günzel das Thema, das die neuen Puppen wie der berühmte rote Faden miteinander verbindet. Ihre Sensibilität beim Aufspüren von Trends ist ihr dabei sehr hilfreich. War es im Jahr 1996 ein winterliches russisches Herrenhaus mit knisterndem Kaminfeuer, so ist es in ihrem Jubiläumsjahr 1997 ein verzauberter englischer Cottage-Garten, in dem sich ihre Puppen aufhalten. „Last days of summer" ist das Thema der Kollektion 1997, zu dem lange vorher Stoffe, Farben und Namen der Puppen ausgesucht wurden. Bei der Wahl der Stoffe läßt sich Hildegard Günzel oft von den Trendsettern des internationalen Interieur-Designs anregen, denn „von ihnen kann man nur lernen". Dazu beobachtet sie die Szene genau. Wenn zum Beispiel „neue Üppigkeit" vorgegeben wird, werden die Kleider ihrer Puppen auch üppiger in Form und Farbe. Denn alle Dinge greifen ineinander, müssen zueinander passen. Harmonie, die Suche nach der vollkommenen Form, sind nach wie vor Antrieb zur Gestaltung der Puppen, und zu diesen gehören schließlich nicht nur

decision which you take also affect others as well as that staff do no automatically have the same ideals as oneself. For this reason I want an informal atmosphere in our company. If all members of staff like me, then I can also motivate them, then they will allow themselves to be infected with my enthusiasm". Sometimes this also works the other way around. A great deal of importance is attached to team spirit in the Günzel doll company, for everyone knows that they need one another to produce the dolls. So it is that lengthy preparations are required until a new collection is ready. First of all Hildegard Günzel finds a theme which links the new dolls like the famous red thread. Her sensitivity for tracking down trends is of great assistance to her for this. If in 1996 it was a wintry Russian manor house with a crackling fire in the hearth, in 1997, Jubilee year, it is an enchanted English cottage-garden, in which her dolls are staying. „Last days of summer" is the theme for the 1997 collection, for which materials, colours, and names for dolls will have been sought out long beforehand. In the selection of materials Hildegard Günzel often allows herself to be inspired by the trend setters of international interior design, „You can but learn from them". She observes the doll scene keenly for trends too. If for example „new opulence" is required, the clothes of her dolls also become more opulent in shape and colour. For everything interacts and must go with everything else. Harmony, the search for perfect form, is still the drive to design dolls and to this ultimately belong not only heads, arms, and legs. Every Günzel doll is a synthesis of the arts. They are sculptures in the best sense. Admittedly you can't play with them, they maintain a certain distance, but they are never cool. They are idealised and privileged little people, beings which touch and like being touched. They seem to be set in motion as if they have been tapped lightly by a fairy's magic wand. Snapshots of a magical world. It is interesting how the dolls are created; Hildegard Günzel's approach is very simi-

Köpfe, Arme und Beine. Jede Günzel-Puppe ist ein Gesamtkunstwerk. Es sind Skulpturen im besten Sinn. Zwar kann man mit ihnen nicht spielen, sie wahren eine gewisse Distanz, lar to that of the Russian icon-painters. At the beginning of the development is the image which Hildegard Günzel has of them, which is then drawn by her. Once she has settled on a

Pandora und Francine, limitiert je 25 Exemplare Europa/USA.
Pandora and Francine. Production limited to 25 samples each in Euro-pe/USA.

doch sind sie niemals kühl. Es sind idealisierte, privilegierte Menschenkinder, Wesen, die berühren und es sich auch gefallen lassen, berührt zu werden. Sie scheinen in der Bewegung zu verharren, wie vom Zauberstab einer Fee touchiert. Momentaufnahmen einer magischen Welt.

Interessant ist, wie die Puppen entstehen. Hildegard Günzel geht dabei ganz ähnlich vor wie die russischen Ikonenmaler.

Am Anfang ihrer Entwicklung steht das Bild, das die Künstlerin von ihnen hat und dann zeichnet. Wenn das Thema gefunden ist, die Auswahl der Stoffe, Farben und Accessoires getroffen wurde, müssen die Puppen, die noch keine sind, einen Namen erhalten. Auch die Namen müssen zum Thema passen, sie sind wichtig. In vielen Kulturen bedeuten sie das Wesen der Personen selbst. Namen beinhalten magische Kräfte. Wenn ein Name zu einer Person nicht paßt, entsteht ein Bruch in der Persönlichkeit, der sich auch Außenstehenden mitteilt. Oftmals werden Günzel-Puppen nach Fertigstellung umbenannt, weil sie sich - eigenwillig, wie sie manchmal sind - mit dem ursprünglich für sie vorgesehenen Namen nicht abfinden wollten. Alle Puppenmacher (und auch Schriftsteller) werden schon Ähnliches erlebt haben.

Anschließend werden die Puppen zu Gruppen zusammengestellt. Sie agieren, kommunizieren miteinander. Vertragen sie sich? Passen sie zusammen? Womit möchten sie spielen? Günzel-Puppen kommen meistens nicht mit leeren Händen. Fast jede Puppe hat irgend ein Spielzeug: Mal sind es Puppen, mal Teddybären, die unter anderem von Carol Ann Stanton für Hildegard Günzel entworfen und angefertigt werden. Erst, wenn die Gruppen „stehen", erhalten die Puppen ihr Gesicht! Dann erst sind sie Personen, Persönlichkeiten. Vielleicht ist dies das Geheimnis, durch das Günzel-Puppen ihre Liebhaber bezaubern: Auch wenn sie häufig in unwirklichen Räumen angesiedelt sind, wirken sie nie verloren, nie wie in einem luftleeren Raum zu Hause. Sie werden von

theme, the selection of materials, colours, and accessories has been made, the dolls, which do not as yet exist, have to be given a name. And the names too must be fitting for the theme, they are important. In many cultures they signify the nature of the person themselves. Names possess magical powers. If a name does not suit a person, a rupture occurs in the personality, and the rupture is conveyed to outsiders too. Günzel dolls are often renamed after completion, because self-willed as they are - they refuse to come to terms with the name originally intended for them. All doll makers (and also writers) will indeed have had a similar experience. Following this the dolls are put together into groups. They act and communicate with each other. Will they get on with each other? Will they go with each other? What will they want to play with? In most cases Günzel dolls do not come empty-handed. Almost every doll has some sort of toy. Sometimes it is a doll, sometimes it is a teddy bear which are designed and produced for Hildegard Günzel by, amongst others, Carol Ann Stanton. Only when the groups have been „assembled" are the dolls given a face ! Only then do they become people, personalities. Perhaps this is the secret with which Günzel dolls cast a spell on their admirers. Even if they are often located in unreal rooms, they never look lost, never like an airless room at home. From the outset they will be „born into" an intact environment, into a family to a certain extent. For this reason the collections never consist of more than ten or twelve dolls at the most. Almost all are limited editions of 70 dolls - 35 for Europe, 35 for the USA (in 1997 only 25 dolls were brought out for Europe and 25 for the USA). Each year there is one very special model of which a maximum of ten dolls are manufactured, sometimes even less. When leaving the Günzel home every doll is accompanied by a video and up-to-date catalogue, as a morning gift. For the last two years the catalogue has included not only pictures of all dolls of the relevant collec-

Unikat, 1997, Unschuld,
Ausstellung „Masterpie-
ces of the world", New
York. Lederbekleidung
Freifrau Isolde von
Malchus.
*Unicum 1997, Innocence,
"Masterpieces of the
world", New York.
Leather apparel made
by Baroness Isolde von
Malchus.*

Anfang an in ein intaktes Umfeld „hineingeboren", gewissermaßen in eine Familie.

Die Kollektionen umfassen deshalb auch nie mehr als zehn, höchstens zwölf Puppen. Fast alle sind auf 70 Exemplare limitiert - 35 für Europa, 35 für die USA (1997 wurden alle Puppen nur jeweils mit 25 Exemplaren für Europa und 25 Exemplaren für die USA herausgebracht). In jedem Jahr ist eine ganz besondere Puppe dabei, von der höchstens zehn Exemplare gefertigt werden, manchmal sogar noch weniger. Jede Günzel-Puppe erhält, wenn sie das Haus verläßt, als Morgengabe ein Video und den aktuellen Katalog, der seit zwei Jahren nicht nur alle Puppen der jeweiligen Kollektion, sondern darüber hinaus auch eine zum Jahresthema passende Geschichte, ein Märchen, enthält, in dem die Puppen vorkommen. Damit werden die Kataloge zu Bilder- und Lesebüchern, die auch nach Ablauf des jeweiligen Kalenderjahres ihren Wert behalten und selbst zu Sammelstücken werden.

25 Jahre Günzel-Puppen. Auch in ihnen kann man lesen wie in einem Buch. Bei einem Vergleich der Puppen läßt sich leicht auch die persönliche Entwicklung der Künstlerin verfolgen. Auch Hildegard Günzel sieht, daß sie ihre privaten Erlebnisse und Erfahrungen in ihren Puppen verarbeitet hat, „doch immer erst hinterher". Sie ist selbstbewußter geworden. „Ich weiß nun, daß ich vieles kann, auch ohne Hilfe, und daß die Welt nicht untergeht, wenn einmal etwas nicht so gut läuft. Ich habe heute mehr Vertrauen, ich vertraue auf die Zukunft und darauf, daß ich auch in unruhigen Zeiten einen ruhigen Weg gehen kann".

Gibt es trotzdem immer noch etwas, was sie gerne einmal machen würde? Hat sie noch Pläne? Träume? Seit das Ehepaar Wohlfarth-Günzel ein englisches Cottage besitzt, hat Hildegard Günzel ihre Liebe zum Garten entdeckt, den sie mit Hingabe bepflanzt. Dafür möchte sie sich gerne an Gartenskulpturen versuchen. Eine Figur, eine in Stein gegossene Elfe, ist bereits fertig. Interessiert sie sich nun

tion, but in addition to this, a story suitable for the theme of the year, a fairy-tale in which the dolls are featured. In this way the catalogues will become picture and story books which will also retain their value after the year they refer to has expired and they will even become collectors' pieces. 25 years of Günzel dolls. They also read like a book. The personal development of the lady artist Hildegard Günzel can also be easily followed with a comparison of dolls. Even Hildegard Günzel sees that she has worked her personal experiences and life into her dolls, but only ever afterwards Hildegard Günzel has become more self-conscious. „Now I know that I can do much without assistance as well, and that the world won't come to an end if something doesn't turn out that well for once, I have more confidence. I have confidence in the future and that even in unsettled times I may tread a peaceful path". In spite of this is there still something that she would like to do? Does she still have plans? Dreams? Since the Wohlfarth-Günzel couple have owned an English cottage, Hildegard Günzel has discovered her love for gardening, which she has taken up with devotion. She would like to try her hand at garden sculptures for this. One figure, an elf cast in stone is already complete. Is she now interested in sculpture? She does find this skill fascinating. „Dolls almost always have bodies made of cloth. Admittedly they can be made all in porcelain, but then they are no longer flexible. It is true that then they do have lovely bodies but you can't dress them as you wish. Anyway what is the point in making a beautiful body for a doll if you are then going to dress it?" Hildegard Günzel would miss the other materials, - silk, lace, fine wool. „There is probably always a small longing in everything that you do which is not satisfied". In spite of this, the future for Hildegard Günzel is becoming visible. Before long she wants to attend a seminar on sculpting. „I want to see, what it's like, taking away instead of putting together, working one's way to the essence of

für Bildhauerei? Dieses Metier findet sie schon faszinierend. „Puppen haben ja fast immer Körper aus Stoff. Man kann sie zwar ganz in Porzellan ausführen, doch dann sind sie nicht mehr beweglich. Sie haben dann zwar schöne Körper, aber die kann man nicht so anziehen, wie ich es möchte. Überhaupt: Warum sollte man einen schönen Akt machen, wenn man ihn anschließend bekleidet?" Sie würde dabei die anderen Materialien - Seide, Spitzen, feine Wolle - vermissen. „Es bleibt wohl immer, bei allem, was man macht, eine kleine Sehnsucht, die nicht befriedigt wird." Trotzdem zeichnet sich der weitere Weg der Künstlerin schon ab: Sie wird demnächst selbst an einem Seminar bei einem Bildhauer teilnehmen. „Ich will sehen, wie das ist, wegzunehmen statt aufzubauen, durch Reduktion zum Wesen des Gegenstandes vorzudringen. - Meine Arbeit, mein Werk darf nicht zu schön, zu glatt werden. Ich möchte noch ein paar Ecken und Kanten haben".

Auch bei Edelsteinen sind es die Facetten, die leuchten.

the object by reduction. My work, my pieces of work mustn't be too beautiful, too smooth. I would like to have a few rough edges".
Even with precious stones it is the facets which light up.

Matthias, Vinyl, 1988   Edith, Vinyl, 1988   Doris, Doty Award, Vinyl, 1988

Classic Children

Auf den folgenden Seiten zeigen wir eine Sammlerübersicht der Vinyl-puppen von Hildegard Günzel. Vinylpuppen sind bei folgenden Firmen erschienen: Classic Children, Alexander Doll Company, Walters-häuser Puppenmanufaktur sowie Hamilton Collection.

On the following pages there is a collector's summary of the vinyl dolls created by Hildegard Günzel. Vinyl dolls have been produced by the following companies :-
Classic Children, Alexandra Doll Company, Waltershäuser Puppen-manufaktur and Hamilton Collection.

Allan, Vinyl, 1988   Wera, Vinyl, 1988   Amanda, Vinyl, 1988

Classic Children, 1989: (von links oben) Muriel, Doll of Excellence 1989, Horst, Rebecca; (von links unten) Melissa, Iris, Dominique.

Classic Children 1989 (from top left). Muriel, Doll of Excellence 1989, Horst, Rebecca (from bottom left) Melissa, Iris, Dominique.

101

Alexander Doll Company

Mai Ling, Vinyl, 1990

Heide, Vinyl, 1990

Tricia, Doll of Excellence, 1990,
Vinyl, 1990

Ushi, Vinyl, 1990

Samantha, Vinyl, 1990

Babsie, Vinyl, 1990

Monica, Vinyl, 1990

Lilian, Porzellan, 1990

Tricia, Porzellan, 1990

Mai Ling, Porzellan, 1990
limit. Edition 500

Hilke, Porzellan, 1990
limit. Edition 500

Samantha, Porzellan, 1990
limit. Edition 500 world wide

◄ Melody with friend,
limitiert 1000 Exem-
plare Porzellan, 1. Ju-
biläumspuppe 1991
mit kleiner Alexander
Puppe im Arm.
*Melody with friend,
production limited to
1000 porcelain samples.
1st jubilee doll 1991
holding a small Alexan-
der doll in its arm*

Heide, Porzellan, 1990
limit. Edition 500

Ebony, Vinyl, 1991

Melody, Vinyl, 1991

Meredith, Vinyl, 1991

Iris, Vinyl, 1991

103

Marissa, Vinyl, 1991   Rebecca, Vinyl, 1991   Karen, Vinyl, 1991

Gruppe (von links): a) Amanda, b) Meryl, c) Erica, d) Dawn, Vinyl, 1991   Blanca, Vinyl, 1991
Group (from left): a. Amanda, b. Meryl, c. Erica, d. Dawn, vinyl, 1991

Xam, Vinyl, 1991   Ginger, Vinyl, 1991   Phoebe, Vinyl, 1991

Courtney, limitiert 1200 Exemplare, Porzellan, 1991
Courtney, production limited to 1200 samples, porcelain, 1991.

(von links) Kimberly, Daphne, Chloe, Kelly, Vinyl, 1991
(from left) Kimberly, Daphne, Chloe, Kelly, vinyl, 1991

(von links) Whitney, Zack, Vinyl, 1992
(from left) Whitney, Zack, vinyl, 1992

(von links) Katie, Jennie, Vinyl, 1992
(from left) Katie, Jennie, vinyl, 1992

Harmony und Cherub, limitiert
1500 Exemplare, Porzellan, 1993
*Harmony and Cherub, production
limited to 1500 samples, porcelain,
1993*

(von links)
Tammy, Teddy,
oben: Alana, Jackie
unten: James,
Lian, Vinyl, 1993
(from left) Tammy,
Teddy
top: Alana, Jackie
bottom: James, Lian,
vinyl, 1993

(von links)
Franny, Willow,
Faith, Annie -
liegend: Baby Love,
Vinyl, 1993
(from left) Franny,
Willow, Faith Annie-
Baby Love, reclining,
vinyl, 1993

(von links) Pablo, Blanca, Vinyl, 1993
(from left) Pablo, Blanca, vinyl, 1993

(von links) Yam, Lotus, Vinyl, 1993
(from left) Yam, Lotus, vinyl, 1993

(von links) Erin, Sally, Vinyl, 1993
(from left) Erin, Sally, vinyl, 1993

(von links) Betsy, Hope, Vinyl, 1993
(from left) Betsy, Hope, vinyl, 1993

(von links) Megan, Brittany
(from left) Megan, Britany

Janna, Jennifer (sitzend), 1994
Janna, Jennifer (seated), 1994

Oben links: Adriana, Corinna (sitzend), 1994
At the top left: Adriana, Corinna (seated), 1994

Waltershäuser Puppenmanufaktur

Waltershäuser dolls manufacturing company

Christine (links Doty Award), Maria, 1995
Christine (left Doty Award), Maria, 1995

(von links) Ilse, Kevin, Margot, 1996
(from left) Ilse, Kevin, Margot, 1996

(von links) Marie Caprice mit Julie im Arm
Carinai mit Tatzel im Arm.
*(from left) Marie Caprice with Julie on her arm
- Carinai with Tatzel on her arm*

Rebecca, 1997

Laurel, Doty Award 1996

Hamilton Collection, USA

Rachel, 1996

113

Valerie, 1997

Sabrina, 1997

Daphne, 1997

Auszeichnungen Hildegard Günzel
Awards won by Hildegard Günzel

1983 1. Preis Gold GDS, Frankfurt/Deutschland
1984 1. Preis Gold „Gold Coast Company", Brisbane/Australien
1984 1. Preis Gold GDS, Luzern/Schweiz
1985 1. Preis Gold GDS, Hamburg/Deutschland
1986 1. Preis Gold GDS, Sydney/Australien
1986 1. Preis Gold GDS, Nelson/New Zealand
1986 „Doty Award" - Doll Reader Magazine / USA
1986 „Doll of Excellence" - Dolls Magazine / USA
1987 „Doll of Excellence" - Dolls Magazine / USA
1987 Nomination „Doty Award" - Doll Reader Magazine / USA
1988 „Doty Award" - Doll Reader Magazine / USA
1988 Nomination „Doll of Excellence" - Dolls Magazine / USA
1989 „Doll of Excellence" - Dolls Magazine / USA
1989 Nomination „Doty Award" - Doll Reader Magazine / USA
1990 „Doll of Excellence" - Dolls Magazine / USA
1990 3 Nominationen „Doty Award" - Doll Reader Magazine / USA
1991 4 Nominationen „Doty Award" - Doll Reader Magazine / USA
1991 „Doty Award" - Doll Reader Magazine / USA für die Puppe „Iris"
1991 „Doty Award" - Doll Reader Magazine / USA für die Puppe „Melody with friend"
1991 „Doll of Excellence" - Dolls Magazine / USA
1992 „Doll of Excellence" - Dolls Magazine / USA für die Puppe „Courtney"
1993 Nomination „Doll of Excellence" - Dolls Magazine / USA
1993 Nomination „Doty Award" - Doll Reader Magazine / USA
1994 „Jumeau"-Preis für das Gesamtwerk - Weltkongreß für Puppensammler und Puppenmacher, Paris/Frankreich
1994 „Jumeau"-Preis für das beste Buch - Weltkongreß für Puppensammler und Puppenmacher, Paris/Frankreich
1994 1. Preis IDEX, Dallas/USA, für die Puppe „Charlotte"
1994 Popular Choice Award GDS für die beste Vinylpuppe, hergestellt von der Waltershäuser Puppenmanufaktur, Waltershausen/Deutschland
1994 Sonderpreis - Verlag Puppen & Spielzeug - beim Jahreskongreß GDS
1994 Nomination „Doty Award" - Doll Reader Magazine / USA
1995 1. Preis IDEX, Dallas/USA, für die Puppe „Keiko"
1995 „IDEX Muse Award", Dallas/USA
1995 Publikumspreis „Der gläserne Feenstab", - Zeitschrift Puppen & Spielzeug, Duisburg/Deutschland
1996 1. Preis IDEX, Dallas/USA, für die Puppe „Elise", (Kat. 'Wax Over Porcelain Dolls')
1996 1. Preis IDEX, Dallas/USA, für die Puppe „Fleurie", (Kat. 'Porcelain Dolls Retailing over $ 1300.00')
1996 1. Preis IDEX, Dallas/USA, für die Puppe „Gaylord", (Kat. 'Ethnic Doll')
1996 1. Preis IDEX, Dallas/USA, für die Puppe „Pauline", (Kat. 'Limit. Edition Doll 35 pieces & under')
1996 1. Preis IDEX, Dallas/USA, für die Bigidurpuppe „Margot", hergestellt von der Waltershäuser Puppenmanufaktur, Waltershausen/Deutschland
1996 1. Preis IDEX, Dallas/USA, für die Bigidurpuppe „Christina", hergestellt von der Waltershäuser Puppenmanufaktur, Waltershausen/Deutschland
1996 Goldmedaille, 2. Internationales Puppen- und Bärenfestival, Gmunden/Österreich, für die Bigidurpuppe „Ilse" hergestellt von der Waltershäuser Puppenmanufaktur, Waltershausen/Deutschland
1996 Nomination „Doty Award" - Doll Reader Magazine / USA, für die Puppe „Pauline"
1996 Nomination „Doll of Excellence" - Dolls Magazine / USA, für die Puppe „Fleurie"
1996 „Doty Award" - Doll Reader Magazine / USA, für die Bigidurpuppe „Christina", hergestellt von der Waltershäuser Puppenmanufaktur, Waltershausen/Deutschland
1996 „Doty Award" - Doll Reader Magazine / USA, für die Puppe „Laurel", hergestellt von der Hamilton-Collection, Jacksonville / USA
1996 „Doll of Excellence" - Dolls Magazine / USA, für die Puppe „Elise"
1996 „Doty Award" - Doll Reader Magazine / USA, für die Puppe „Lara"
1997 1. Preis IDEX, Dallas/USA, für die Puppe „Eleanor", (Kat. 'Wax Over Porcelain Dolls')
1997 1. Preis IDEX, Dallas/USA, für die Puppe „Imogene", (Kat. 'Limit. Edition Doll 35 pieces & under')
1997 Nomination „Doty Award" - Doll Reader Magazine / USA, für die Puppe „Carinai", hergestellt von der Waltershäuser Puppenmanufaktur, Waltershausen/Deutschland
1997 Nomination „Doty Award" - Doll Reader Magazine / USA, für die Puppe „Francine"
1997 Nomination „Doty Award" - Doll Reader Magazine / USA, für die Puppe „Pandora"
1997 Nomination „Dolls of Excellence" - Doll Magazine / USA, für die Puppe „Florence"
1997 Nomination „Dolls of Excellence" - Doll Magazine / USA, für die Puppe „Marie-Caprice", hergestellt von der Waltershäuser Puppenmanufaktur, Waltershausen/Deutschland

1983 1. Prize Gold GDS, Frankfurt/Germany
1984 1. Prize Gold „Gold Coast Company", Brisbane/Australia
1984 1. Prize Gold GDS, Luzern/Switzerland
1985 1. Prize Gold GDS, Hamburg/Germany
1986 1. Prize Gold GDS, Sidney/Australia
1986 1. Prize Gold GDS, Nelson/New Zealand
1986 „Doty Award" - Doll Reader Magazine / USA
1986 „Doll of Excellence" - Dolls Magazine / USA
1987 „Doll of Excellence" - Dolls Magazine / USA
1987 Nomination „Doty Award" - Doll Reader Magazine / USA
1988 „Doty Award" - Doll Reader Magazine / USA
1988 Nomination „Doll of Excellence" - Dolls Magazine / USA
1989 „Doll of Excellence" - Dolls Magazine / USA
1989 Nomination „Doty Award" - Doll Reader Magazine / USA
1990 „Doll of Excellence" - Doll Magazine / USA
1990 3 Nominationen „Doty Award" - Doll Reader Magazine / USA
1991 4 Nominationen „Doty Award" - Doll Reader Magazine / USA
1991 „Doty Award" - Doll Reader Magazine / USA for the doll „Iris"
1991 „Doty Award" - Doll Reader Magazine / USA for the doll „Melody with friend"
1991 Nomination „Doll of Excellence" - Dolls Magazine / USA
1992 „Doll of Excellence" - Dolls Magazine / USA for the doll „Courtney"
1993 Nomination „Doll of Excellence" - Dolls Magazine / USA
1993 Nomination „Doty Award" - Doll Reader Magazine / USA
1994 „Jumeau"-Prize for her entire work - Weltkongreß für Puppensammler und Puppenmacher, Paris/France
1994 „Jumeau"-Prize for the best book - Weltkongreß für Puppensammler und Puppenmacher, Paris/France
1994 1. Prize IDEX, Dallas/USA, for the doll „Charlotte"
1994 Popular Choice Award GDS for the best Vinyl-doll, manufactured by Waltershäuser Puppenmanufaktur, Waltershausen/Germany
1994 Special Award - Verlag Puppen & Spielzeug - at the Congreß of the GDS
1994 Nomination „Doty Award" - Doll Reader Magazine / USA
1995 1. Prize IDEX, Dallas/USA, for the doll „Keiko"
1995 „IDEX Muse Award", Dallas/USA
1995 Special Award „Der gläserne Feenstab", - Magazine Puppen & Spielzeug, Duisburg/Germany
1996 1. Prize IDEX, Dallas/USA, for the doll „Elise", (Cat. 'Wax Over Porcelain Dolls')
1996 1. Prize IDEX, Dallas/USA, for the doll „Fleurie", (Cat. 'Porcelain Dolls Retailing over $ 1300.00')
1996 1. Prize IDEX, Dallas/USA, for the doll „Gaylord", (Cat. 'Ethnic Doll')
1996 1. Prize IDEX, Dallas/USA, for the doll „Pauline", (Cat. 'Limit. Edition Doll 35 pieces & under')
1996 1. Prize IDEX, Dallas/USA, for the Bigidur-doll „Margot", manufactured by Waltershäuser Puppenmanufaktur, Waltershausen/Germany
1996 1. Prize IDEX, Dallas/USA, for the Bigidur-doll „Christina", manufactured by Waltershäuser Puppenmanufaktur, Waltershausen/Germany
1996 Medal in Gold, 2. Internationales Puppen- und Bärenfestival, Gmunden/Austria, for the Bigidurdoll „Ilse" manufactured by Waltershäuser Puppenmanufaktur, Waltershausen/Germany
1996 Nomination „Doty Award" - Doll Reader Magazine / USA, for the doll „Pauline"
1996 Nomination „Doll of Excellence" - Dolls Magazine / USA, for the doll „Fleurie"
1996 „Doty Award" - Doll Reader Magazine / USA, for the Bigidur-doll „Christina", manufactured by Waltershäuser Puppenmanufaktur, Waltershausen/Germany
1996 „Doty Award" - Doll Reader Magazine / USA, for the doll „Laurel", manufactured by The Hamilton-Collection, Jacksonville / USA
1996 „Doll of Excellence" - Dolls Magazine / USA, for the doll „Elise"
1996 „Doty Award" - Doll Reader Magazine / USA, for the doll „Lara"
1997 1. Prize IDEX, Dallas/USA, for the doll „Eleanor", (Cat. 'Wax Over Porcelain Dolls')
1997 1. Prize IDEX, Dallas/USA, for the doll „Imogene", (Cat. 'Limited Edition Doll 35 pieces & under')
1997 Nomination „Doty Award" - Doll Reader Magazine / USA, for the Bigidur-doll „Carinai", manufactured by Waltershäuser Puppenmanufaktur, Waltershausen/Germany
1997 Nomination „Doty Award" - Doll Reader Magazine / USA, for the doll „Francine"
1997 Nomination „Doty Award" - Doll Reader Magazine / USA, for the doll „Pandora"
1997 Nomination „Doll of Excellence" - Dolls Magazine / USA, for the doll „Florence"
1997 Nomination „Doll of Excellence" - Dolls Magazine / USA, for the Bigidur-doll „Marie-Caprice", manufactured by Waltershäuser Puppenmanufaktur, Waltershausen/Germany

Bücher aus dem
Verlag Puppen & Spielzeug

Max Kruse
Die verwandelte Zeit
Der Aufbau der Käthe-Kruse-Werkstätte in Bad Pyrmont

Max Kruse, Sohn der Puppenkünstlerin Käthe Kruse, erinnert sich an sein Leben im Deutschland der Nachkriegsjahre.

200 Seiten, Bildtafeln, Format 14,5 cm x 21 cm, gebunden, ISBN 3-87463-237-7

Christa Langer
Das Glückskind
Käthe Kruse und ihre Werkstatt in Bad Pyrmont

Wichtige Jahre in der Firmengeschichte Käthe Kruses werden zusammenfassend dargestellt und die Puppen in einem umfangreichen Bildteil gezeigt.

Zahlr. Farbabb., 56 Seiten, gebunden, Format 19,5 cm x 23 cm, ISBN 3-87463-180-x

Gabriele Bothen-Hack / Karin Schrey
Das Puppenparadies
Puppen von 1880 - 1920

Lassen Sie sich vom Teddy „Primus" in das Puppenparadies entführen. Die Autorinnen haben eine wohlgehütete Puppensammlung von musealem Wert entdeckt und stellen diese exquisiten Antikpuppen zum ersten Mal vor.

108 Seiten, 75 farbige Abbildungen, Format 24,5 cm x 31 cm, gebunden, ISBN 3-87463-183-4

Karin Schmidt
Seelenzauber
Puppenkinder dieser Erde

Die bekannte Puppenkünstlerin Karin Schmidt stellt ihre Puppenkinder aus der ganzen Welt vor, die teils nach lebenden Vorbildern, teils nach eigener Phantasie modelliert sind.

80 Seiten, gebunden, Format 24 cm x 30,5 cm, ISBN 3-87463-250-4

Carin Lossnitzer
Puppenspielen, Puppensammeln, Puppenmachen
Bekannt wurde Carin Lossnitzer mit ihren CARLOS-Puppen, die ersten von Künstlerhand entworfenen, industriell hergestellten Vinylpuppen für Sammler.

*64 Seiten, 45 farbige Abbildungen, **dt./engl. Texte**, Format 23,5 cm x 27,5 cm, gebunden, ISBN 3-87463-201-6*

Christiane Gräfnitz
Deutsche Papiermaché Puppen
1760 - 1860

Erstmals wird das faszinierende Gebiet der Puppen aus Papiermaché umfassend dokumentiert. Die Autorin gibt Aufschluß über die Zusammensetzung des Werkstoffes, die Entwicklung des Produktionsprozesses sowie eine Charakteristik der wichtigsten Hersteller und die Merkmale ihrer Puppen.

108 Seiten, zahlreiche farbige und Schwarzweiß-Abbildungen, Format 24,5 cm x 31 cm, gebunden, ISBN 3-87463-206-7

Auch in englischer Sprache erschienen

Christa Langer
Charakterpuppen
Vom Portrait zum Modell

Anhand bisher unveröffentlichter Dokumente und neuer Fotos werden die Vorbilder einer ganzen Reihe von Charakterpuppenmodellen bestimmt und die Künstler mit ihrer Arbeit vorgestellt.

*108 Seiten, 60 farbige und und 50 s/w-Abbildungen, **deutsch/englische Texte**, gebunden, Format 24,5 cm x 31 cm, ISBN 3-87463-200-8*

Hildegard Wegner
Schatten ohne Licht
„Puppen" und Fotografien

Das Außer-Gewöhnliche, das sich nicht der Norm anpassen kann oder will, zieht die Aufmerksamkeit und Anteilnahme der Künstlerin Hildegard Wegner an.

*72 Seiten, zahlreiche Abbildungen, gebunden, **deutsch/englische Texte**, Format 24 cm x 30,5 cm, ISBN 3-87463-240-7*